Foreign Trade Regimes and Economic Development:
THE PHILIPPINES

Foreign Trade Regimes and Economic Development:

A Special Conference Series on Foreign Trade Regimes and Economic Development

VOLUME V

NATIONAL BUREAU OF ECONOMIC RESEARCH
New York   1975

THE PHILIPPINES

by **Robert E. Baldwin**

UNIVERSITY OF WISCONSIN

DISTRIBUTED BY Columbia University Press
New York and London

NATIONAL BUREAU OF ECONOMIC RESEARCH

*A Special Conference Series on Foreign Trade Regimes
and Economic Development*

Library of Congress Card Number: 74–82373
ISBN for the series: 0–87014–500–2
ISBN for this volume: 0–87014–505–3

Printed in the United States of America
DESIGNED BY JEFFREY M. BARRIE

Relation of the Directors of the National Bureau to
Publication of the Country Studies in the Series on
Foreign Trade Regimes and Economic Development

The individual country studies have not passed through the National Bureau's normal procedures for review and approval of research reports by the Board of Directors. In view of the way in which these studies were planned and reviewed at successive working parties of authors and Co-Directors, the National Bureau's Executive Committee has approved their publication in a manner analogous to conference proceedings, which are exempted from the rules governing submission of manuscripts to, and critical review by, the Board of Directors. *It should therefore be understood that the views expressed herein are those of the authors only and do not necessarily reflect those of the National Bureau or its Board of Directors.*

The synthesis volumes in the series, prepared by the Co-Directors of the project, are subject to the normal procedures for review and approval by the Directors of the National Bureau.

Contents

Tables

CHART   xi

Chart

Co-Directors' Foreword

This volume is one of a series resulting from the research project on Exchange Control, Liberalization, and Economic Development sponsored by the National Bureau of Economic Research, the name of the project having been subsequently broadened to Foreign Trade Regimes and Economic Development. Underlying the project was the belief by all participants that the phenomena of exchange control and liberalization in less developed countries require careful and detailed analysis within a sound theoretical framework, and that the effects of individual policies and restrictions cannot be analyzed without consideration of both the nature of their administration and the economic environment within which they are adopted as determined by the domestic economic policy and structure of the particular country.

The research has thus had three aspects: (1) development of an analytical framework for handling exchange control and liberalization; (2) within that framework, research on individual countries, undertaken independently by senior scholars; and (3) analysis of the results of these independent efforts with a view to identifying those empirical generalizations that appear to emerge from the experience of the countries studied.

The analytical framework developed in the first stage was extensively commented upon by those responsible for the research on individual countries, and was then revised to the satisfaction of all participants. That framework, serving as the common basis upon which the country studies were undertaken, is further reflected in the syntheses reporting on the third aspect of the research.

The analytical framework pinpointed these three principal areas of research which all participants undertook to analyze for their own countries.

Subject to a common focus on these three areas, each participant enjoyed maximum latitude to develop the analysis of his country's experience in the way he deemed appropriate. Comparison of the country volumes will indicate that this freedom was indeed utilized, and we believe that it has paid handsome dividends. The three areas singled out for in-depth analysis in the country studies are:

1. *The anatomy of exchange control:* The economic efficiency and distributional implications of alternative methods of exchange control in each country were to be examined and analyzed. Every method of exchange control differs analytically in its effects from every other. In each country study care has been taken to bring out the implications of the particular methods of control used. We consider it to be one of the major results of the project that these effects have been brought out systematically and clearly in analysis of the individual countries' experience.

2. *The liberalization episode:* Another major area for research was to be a detailed analysis of attempts to liberalize the payments regime. In the analytical framework, devaluation and liberalization were carefully distinguished, and concepts for quantifying the extent of devaluation and of liberalization were developed. It was hoped that careful analysis of individual devaluation and liberalization attempts, both successful and unsuccessful, would permit identification of the political and economic ingredients of an effective effort in that direction.

3. *Growth relationships:* Finally, the relationship of the exchange control regime to growth via static-efficiency and other factors was to be investigated. In this regard, the possible effects on savings, investment allocation, research and development, and entrepreneurship were to be highlighted.

In addition to identifying the three principal areas to be investigated, the analytical framework provided a common set of concepts to be used in the studies and distinguished various phases regarded as useful in tracing the experience of the individual countries and in assuring comparability of the analyses. The concepts are defined and the phases delineated in Appendix C.

The country studies undertaken within this project and their authors are as follows:

Brazil	Albert Fishlow, University of California, Berkeley
Chile	Jere R. Behrman, University of Pennsylvania
Colombia	Carlos F. Diaz-Alejandro, Yale University
Egypt	Bent Hansen, University of California, Berkeley, and Karim Nashashibi, International Monetary Fund
Ghana	J. Clark Leith, University of Western Ontario

India	Jagdish N. Bhagwati, Massachusetts Institute of Technology, and T. N. Srinivasan, Indian Statistical Institute
Israel	Michael Michaely, The Hebrew University of Jerusalem
Philippines	Robert E. Baldwin, University of Wisconsin
South Korea	Charles R. Frank, Jr., Princeton University and The Brookings Institution; Kwang Suk Kim, Korea Development Institute, Republic of Korea; and Larry E. Westphal, Northwestern University
Turkey	Anne O. Krueger, University of Minnesota

The principal results of the different country studies are brought together in our overall syntheses. Each of the country studies, however, has been made self-contained, so that readers interested in only certain of these studies will not be handicapped.

In undertaking this project and bringing it to successful completion, the authors of the individual country studies have contributed substantially to the progress of the whole endeavor, over and above their individual research. Each has commented upon the research findings of other participants, and has made numerous suggestions which have improved the overall design and execution of the project. The country authors who have collaborated with us constitute an exceptionally able group of development economists, and we wish to thank all of them for their cooperation and participation in the project.

We must also thank the National Bureau of Economic Research for its sponsorship of the project and its assistance with many of the arrangements necessary in an undertaking of this magnitude. Hal B. Lary, Vice President-Research, has most energetically and efficiently provided both intellectual and administrative input into the project over a three-year period. We would also like to express our gratitude to the Agency for International Development for having financed the National Bureau in undertaking this project. Michael Roemer and Constantine Michalopoulos particularly deserve our sincere thanks.

JAGDISH N. BHAGWATI
Massachusetts Institute of Technology

ANNE O. KRUEGER
University of Minnesota

Preface

The objectives of this book are twofold: to present an analysis of trade and payments policies in the Philippines that, it is hoped, can contribute to the formulation of better future policies for that country; and, as one of a series of country studies in a larger project, to provide background material within a common framework that can be utilized to understand better the reasons for the relative success or failure of various exchange-rate and trade policies in a wide range of economic circumstances and environments.[1]

The pursuit of the two goals simultaneously has, I believe, contributed positively toward the achievement of each. In having as a sole objective the evaluation of past policies in a specific country for the purpose of recommending policies that apply to that country, one is likely not only to adopt a parochial approach but to present conclusions based on material that is not always explicitly set forth in the study. The reader who is not an expert in the subject can do little else but agree with the author, since the data that are presented are highly selective and closely interwoven with the author's conclusions. However, given the second objective as well, it is necessary to recount in some detail the nature of the trade and payments policies adopted by the Philippines in such a way that the author's opinions do not always intrude, and so that the reader will be able to draw his own conclusions about the lessons to be learned from various economic events. The acquisition of economic knowledge is hampered because many studies present too few facts about what went on, and too many conclusions that are not carefully substantiated. Those interested in improving policymaking thus frequently find they must cover ground already studied by others to satisfy themselves that the conclusions reached by other writers are pertinent to the particular problems in which they are interested.

On the other hand, if the only purpose of a monograph is to provide inputs into a broader integrating study, one is likely to describe and analyze a country's experience with different foreign trade regimes in an overly stylized manner that fails to capture the unique economic, political, and social conditions existing in the country. Without an understanding of these latter features, any policy recommendations directed at the particular country may well be unrealistic or not meaningful.

In consequence of the two goals I have made a deliberate effort to present a somewhat detailed description of Philippine trade and payment policies without drawing economic conclusions at every step of the way. Chapters 2, 3, and 4 are largely of this nature, although Chapter 3 does have a section in which I evaluate the exchange-decontrol efforts of the early 1960s. The detail given in these chapters is excessive for readers interested in a general survey of the foreign trade regimes followed by the Philippines, and they are advised to focus on the tables given in these chapters, summarizing major policy actions. Those readers interested in an in-depth understanding of the country's international economic policies (and this is the audience to which the study is primarily directed) will, it is hoped, not find the enumeration of these policies too overwhelming. Its purpose is to permit the reader himself to make an informed judgment about the merits or drawbacks of the various policies adopted.

In Chapter 5 I try to help in the formation of this judgment by presenting a quantitative assessment of the different aspects of foreign trade regimes in which such concepts as effective rates of exchange, implicit levels of protection, and effective rates of protection are utilized. Finally in Chapter 6 an evaluation is made of the country's international economic policies in terms of economic efficiency, growth rates, and consequences on the distribution of income. This is done not only by drawing on the preceding historical and quantitative analyses, but by attempting to integrate previous studies of trade and payments policies in the Philippines.

I have become indebted to many people in the course of the study. First, I am grateful to the Agency for International Development (AID) for providing financial support for undertaking the study and to the National Bureau of Economic Research for administering the grant and providing funds to publish the monograph. Jagdish Bhagwati and Anne Krueger, the entrepreneurs of the general project, are to be thanked not only for securing the financial support but together with Hal Lary, Charles Frank, and Carlos Díaz-Alejandro for reading the manuscript and providing many valuable suggestions. I am also greatly indebted to the members of the Economics Department at the University of the Philippines, especially Amado Castro, José Encarnación, and Leon Mears. Without the advice of these individuals and their co-operation in providing the physical facilities for carrying out the study as well as introductions to government and business officials, the study could not have been done. But more than this, the economists at the University of the Philippines are a highly motivated, research-oriented group who have written extensively about the Philippine economy. I have profited enormously from reading their books and papers and discussing my project with them.

Two able research assistants, Rosalinda Marquez in Manila and Juliet Mak in Madison, have been extremely helpful in searching out data on the Philippine economy and in undertaking statistical analyses of this data. Typing assistance has been provided by Roberta Wood, Mary Boudreau, Margaret Burns, Jeanine Gleason, and Jo Ann Giese. The chart was drawn by H. Irving Forman, and the manuscript was edited by Ester Moskowitz.

1. This broader study is being carried out by Jagdish N. Bhagwati and Anne O. Krueger.

Principal Dates and Historical Events in the Philippines

1946   The Philippines achieve independence.

Enactment of the Bell Trade Act providing for an eight-year period of free trade between the United States and the Philippines and then a gradual increase in the share of regular duties that each country would pay.

Passage of an act granting special internal tax privileges to "new and necessary" industries.

1949   Emergence of a foreign-exchange crisis and the introduction of exchange controls.

1951   Imposition of a 17 per cent excise tax on the peso value of foreign exchange sold by the banking system.

1953   Enactment of a new tax exemption law for "new and necessary" industries, covering import taxes as well as internal taxes.

1955   Signing of the Laurel-Langley Agreement between the United States and the Philippines, providing for an acceleration of the rate at which imports from the United States would be subject to the full amounts of Philippine tariffs.

Replacement of the 17 per cent excise tax on foreign exchange by a gradually declining tax on imports.

1957   Passage of an act raising Philippine tariffs.

1959   Introduction of a 25 per cent margin fee levied by the Central Bank on sales of foreign exchange.

1960   Beginning of the decontrol period with the establishment of a multiple exchange-rate system.

1961   Passage of another tax-exemption law favoring many domestic manufacturing industries.

1962   Removal of exchange controls and move to a uniform exchange rate for all transactions except exports.

1965   Elimination of penalty exchange rate for exporters.

1967   Introduction of some controls over foreign-exchange transactions. Passage of the Investment Incentive Act granting special tax privileges to key domestic industries.

1970   Floating of the peso after the emergence of a foreign-exchange crisis. Passage of the Export Incentives Act designed to stimulate new export industries.

Foreign Trade Regimes and Economic Development:
THE PHILIPPINES

Chapter 1

An Overview of the Philippine Economy and Its Foreign Trade Regimes

The main purpose of this study is to examine the effects on growth, resource allocation, and income distribution of the various exchange controls and commercial policies utilized by the Philippine government from the end of World War II through 1971. Special attention is devoted to assessing the efforts to liberalize exchange controls. Since trade and payments policies are only one means (although a very important one) employed by governments in pursuit of their goals of growth, resource allocation, and income distribution, it is also necessary to consider the role of other major policy tools in that pursuit. In particular, the fiscal and monetary measures that accompanied shifts in trade and payments policies will be examined in order to place the latter in their proper perspective.

To provide a general perspective for the subsequent detailed description and analysis of the exchange controls and related measures employed between 1946 and 1971, a brief overview is presented in this chapter first, of the nature of the Philippine economy, and second, of the various exchange-control phases through which the economy has moved during those years.

THE STRUCTURE OF THE PHILIPPINE ECONOMY

A unique geographical feature of the Philippines is that the country consists of some seven thousand islands stretching over an area of more than a thousand miles from north to south and about seven hundred miles from east to

1

west. However, the combined land area of the islands is only 115,000 square miles. The country's population in 1971 was 37 million. This is roughly comparable to that of such other countries in Southeast Asia and the Far East as Thailand (34 million), Burma (28 million), and South Korea (32 million). The population density of the Philippines is, however, greater than that of any other Southeast Asian country except Singapore.[1] Like several countries in this region, the rate of population growth in the Philippines has averaged about 3 per cent annually since 1950.

The per capita gross domestic product of $179 in 1970 places the Philippines among the lower half of all developing countries in the world, but among the highest of the developing countries in South Asia, Southeast Asia, and the Far East.[2] For example, 1970 per capita gross domestic product (GDP) in Thailand was $174; in Indonesia, $70; in India, $91; in South Korea, $257; and in Taiwan, $414.[3] The country's average annual growth of real GDP of 5.9 per cent from 1961 to 1970 was somewhat higher than the average for all developing countries during this decade, but within Southeast Asia and the Far East such countries as Thailand, Malaysia, Singapore, South Korea, and Taiwan grew at a faster pace.

The growth pattern of Philippine gross domestic product and of net domestic product and its components during various subperiods between 1946 and 1971 is indicated by the data in Table 1-1. As is shown in this table and in Chart 1-1, the average annual growth rate of gross national product was very rapid during the reconstruction period in the latter part of the 1940s, and also was quite high during the early period of import-substitution policies in the first half of the 1950s. A slowdown to a 5 per cent annual growth rate occurred in the last part of the decade, but this was reversed in the 1960s as the average rate rose to 5.6 per cent and 6.0 per cent annually in the next two periods. Manufacturing activity also expanded very quickly during the reconstruction period, and this growth continued at an annual rate of more than 12 per cent from 1951 to 1955. The pace of development in this sector not only then declined to 7.7 per cent annually in the 1956–60 period, but the fall continued, reaching an average annual growth rate of 4.0 per cent in the next five-year period. However, the rate rose from 1966 to 1971 to 5.9 per cent.

The rapid rate of growth in manufacturing resulted in an increase in the share of this sector in net domestic product from 10.7 per cent in 1948 to 17.9 per cent by 1960. Between 1960 and 1971, however, the relative share failed to increase further and stood at 17.6 per cent in 1971.

As is indicated by the data in Table 1-2, one result of the increase in the relative importance of the manufacturing sector has been a sharp decline between the end of the 1940s and the early 1970s in the share of imports consisting of simple manufactures and foodstuffs. On the other hand, the import share of such items as machinery and transportation equipment as well as

TABLE 1-1

Average Annual Net Domestic Product by Industry, Average Annual Gross National Product, and Population, 1946–71

	1946–50	1951–55	1956–60	1961–65	1966–71
Agriculture, fishery, and forestry					
Value[a]	1,619	2,407	2,981	3,574	4,774
Growth rate[b]	12.4	7.2	3.0	4.2	5.7
Mining and quarrying					
Value[a]	41	100	148	176	365
Growth rate[b]	70.3	12.0	8.4	4.5	19.9
Manufacturing					
Value[a]	440	1,000	1,609	2,058	2,672
Growth rate[b]	50.5	12.1	7.7	4.0	5.9
Construction					
Value[a]	323	346	370	422	489
Growth rate[b]	38.1	−2.7	0.3	8.0	−1.9
All other					
Value[a]	1,760	2,924	4,146	5,407	7,138
Growth rate[b]	16.9	9.1	5.9	5.5	5.2
Net domestic product					
Value[a]	4,194	6,776	9,255	11,637	15,399
Growth rate[b]	18.9	8.1	5.0	5.0	5.4
Gross national product					
Value[a]	4,700	7,619	10,420	13,398	18,207
Growth rate[b]	19.9	8.1	5.0	5.6	6.0
Population					
Thousands	19,044	21,886	25,435	29,526	34,941
Growth rate[b]	2.3	3.1	3.1	3.0	3.0
Per capita GNP					
Value[a]	246	347	409	453	522
Growth rate[b]	17.1	4.9	1.9	2.1	2.9

SOURCE:
Income data: 1948–67—National Economic Council, *Statistical Reporter*, January–March 1969, pp. 12–13 and 19; 1968–70—National Economic Council, *Statistical Reporter*, April–June 1971; 1971—National Economic Council.

Population: 1946–59—Bureau of Census and Statistics, *Handbook of Philippine Statistics*, 1960 and 1963; 1960–71—Bureau of Census and Statistics.

a. Average annual level in millions of pesos at 1955 prices.

b. Average annual percentage rate of growth.

CHART 1-1

Macroeconomic Indicators and Phases, the Philippines, 1946–71

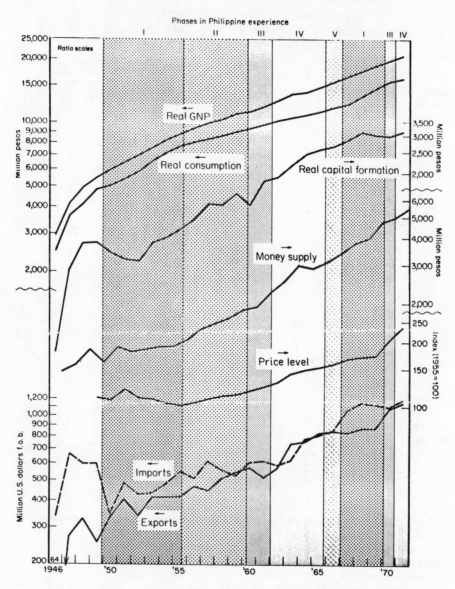

SOURCE: Real GNP, real consumption, and real capital formation for 1946–70 from National Economic Council, *The Statistical Reporter*, January–March 1969 and April–June 1971; 1971 from National Economic Council, "The Gross National Product and National Income of the Philippines, Calendar Year 1969 to Calendar Year 1971," mimeographed; real values are expressed in 1955 prices. Money supply, price level, imports, and exports from Central Bank of the Philippines, *Statistical Bulletin*, December 1971.

TABLE 1-2

Philippine Imports, 1949–71

Percentage Distribution

Year	Total (mill. U.S. dol.)	Food	Beverages and Tobacco	Crude Materials	Mineral Fuels	Chemicals	Animal and Vegetable Oil	Mfrd. Goods Classified by Materials	Misc. Mfrd.	Machinery and Transport. Equip.	Misc. Commodities
1949	586	25.3	3.4	0.6	6.0	6.0	.4	37.6	7.9	12.8	0.04
1952	421	18.2	4.7	1.2	9.9	7.7	.2	37.2	5.5	15.2	0.01
1953	452	17.0	3.4	1.3	10.8	8.5	.4	36.9	5.0	16.7	0.05
1954	479	16.5	2.3	1.2	11.3	8.0	.4	36.3	5.7	18.2	0.10
1955	548	18.7	2.9	1.6	9.8	8.0	.3	34.9	4.4	19.0	0.4
1956	506	17.4	1.4	2.3	10.4	7.7	.4	32.2	3.2	24.8	0.1
1957	613	17.6	0.3	2.9	9.4	9.3	.4	33.5	3.3	23.0	0.2
1958	559	21.0	0.6	4.0	10.9	9.2	.4	27.7	3.1	22.6	0.3
1959	524	13.0	0.5	5.1	11.4	11.2	.5	26.4	2.9	28.5	0.4
1960	604	14.1	0.1	5.4	9.9	9.1	.4	21.7	2.8	36.0	0.4
1961	611	16.6	0.1	6.0	8.1	10.1	.4	21.7	2.8	33.4	0.7
1962	587	14.9	0.3	6.9	10.2	10.4	.6	20.6	3.0	32.3	0.7
1963	618	16.9	0.3	6.2	10.0	8.9	.6	19.1	3.0	33.8	1.2
1964	780	15.7	0.2	5.3	9.9	9.0	.6	19.7	3.0	35.1	1.5
1965	808	19.2	0.3	4.4	9.5	9.0	.5	18.7	2.6	34.2	1.8
1966	853	14.4	0.5	6.0	9.9	9.2	.5	20.8	2.7	34.8	1.3
1967	1,062	15.1	0.6	4.2	8.8	9.1	.4	19.9	2.5	38.3	1.2
1968	1,150	11.5	0.7	5.9	9.2	9.5	.4	20.3	2.8	38.5	1.1
1969	1,131	11.0	1.0	5.2	9.4	10.0	.4	20.4	2.7	39.2	0.6
1970	1,090	9.6	0.7	5.5	10.9	11.6	.4	21.7	2.5	36.7	0.4
1971	1,186	12.3	0.5	5.6	11.9	12.2	.5	16.5	2.6	37.4	0.4

SOURCE: Central Bank of the Philippines, *Annual Report* for various years.

various raw materials expanded significantly, reflecting Philippine industrialization efforts.

The share of agricultural, fishing, and forestry activity in net domestic
product during the postwar period followed a path roughly inverse to that
for manufacturing, falling from 38.2 per cent in 1948 to 31.4 per cent in
1960. In 1971, it was 30.6 per cent. As is typical in developing countries,
the share of the labor force employed in agriculture is much larger than the
share of agriculture in net domestic product. In 1948, the labor force share
for agriculture was 71.5 per cent, whereas in 1971 it was 56.0 per cent. Manufacturing absorbed 6.6 per cent of the labor force in 1948 and 11 per cent
in 1971.

The importance of the agricultural sector in the Philippine economy is
reflected in the composition of the country's exports. As is indicated by the
data in Table 1-3, seven of the ten leading exports are crude or simply processed agricultural commodities, namely, copra, sugar, desiccated coconut,
coconut oil, copra meal, canned pineapples, and bananas. The other three
items—logs and lumber, plywood, and copper concentrates—are forest or
mineral products. (See Chart 1-1 for the behavior of total exports and imports
over time.) These latter exports reflect the rich endowment of forest and mineral resources in the country. In the mid 1950s more than 60 per cent of the
total land area was covered by forests, and logs and lumber have been the
fastest growing export items during the period covered by this study. Copper
mining is by far the most significant activity in mining and quarrying, contributing 75 per cent to the net value added of this sector; but gold mining,
iron ore mining, and chromium ore mining also are moderately important. In
addition, manganese ore, mercury, lead, silver, zinc, and molybdenum are
mined.

Table 1-4 contains data for the components of the Philippines' balance
of payments for various subperiods. The average annual growth rate of exports of goods (in constant prices) over the entire period from 1949 to 1971
was 5.8 per cent. Between 1950 and 1955, the rate was 7.4 per cent; between
1955 and 1960, it was 4.5 per cent; between 1960 and 1965, 7.1 per cent;
and between 1965 and 1971, 4.7 per cent. The share of exports of goods
and services in real gross national product was 14.5 per cent as of 1971 (see
Table 1-5)—about the same as in 1952. The openness of the economy in
terms of exports is roughly comparable to that of Thailand, but considerably
less than either Malaysia or Taiwan.

It is also brought out in Table 1-5 that gross domestic capital formation
is a significant share of gross national product, an important finding. The 19.5
per cent level in 1971 is comparable to the level in such industrial countries as
the United Kingdom and Italy and only about three percentage points less
than that in Taiwan and Thailand. The steady rise in this figure from around

12 per cent in the early 1950s to its present level is one of the more important economic changes that has taken place in the Philippines over the last twenty years (see Chart 1-1).

In 1969 the per capita official flow of external resources to the Philippines amounted to $3.72. This flow was higher than to Thailand ($2.59), Indonesia ($3.13), or Pakistan ($3.37), but less than to South Korea ($12.72) or Ceylon ($4.00).[4] Foreign aid was much more important in the late 1940s and early 1950s, however. Approximately $1.2 billion of rehabilitation aid was furnished by the U.S. government between 1944 and 1950.[5] Between 1951 and 1956 U.S. economic aid amounted to $171 million and was equivalent to 28 per cent of the investment expenditures of the Philippine government.[6]

Compared to many developing countries, the role of the Philippine government in economic activities has been moderate. Total government expenditures in 1970 were equal to 11.3 per cent of the gross national product in that year. Comparable percentages for other countries at about this time were 20 per cent for Thailand, 24 per cent for Malaysia, 16 per cent for India, and 19 per cent for South Korea.[7]

Although the ratio of government expenditures to GNP has remained roughly the same since the late 1940s, there has been an important shift in the method of financing these expenditures. In 1950 indirect taxes (less subsidies) amounted to 47 per cent of government current receipts, while direct taxes and current transfer payments from abroad were 10 per cent and 39 per cent, respectively.[8] In 1970 the indirect and direct tax components had risen to 68 per cent and 22 per cent, respectively, while foreign transfer payments contributed only 4 per cent.

The inflation record of the Philippines is reasonably good in comparison to many other developing countries. Between 1963 and 1970, for example, wholesale prices rose 45 per cent in the Philippines in contrast to 66 per cent in India, 116 per cent in South Korea, 46 per cent in Turkey, 565 per cent in Chile, and 802 per cent in Brazil. On the other hand, the wholesale price rise during these years was only 7 per cent in Taiwan, 33 per cent in Egypt, 22 per cent in Mexico, and 17 per cent in Thailand.[9] The average annual increase in wholesale prices in the Philippines between 1949 and 1970 was 3.2 per cent. Most of the rise in prices between these years occurred in the 1960s (see Chart 1-1).

As will be explained in more detail in later chapters, monetary policy has often been used to improve the re-election prospects of a particular administration, as well as for furthering the goals of economic development. Between 1949 and 1970, the average annual increase in the money supply was 7.6 per cent (Chart 1-1). The government likewise incurred budgetary deficits for both short-run political purposes and longer-run economic functions. The

TABLE 1-3

Philippine Exports,[a] **1949–71**
(millions of U.S. dollars)

Year	Total Exports	Exports of Principal Commodities[b]	Copra	Sugar	Abaca	Logs and Lumber	Desic- cated Coconut
1949	247.9	188.3	89.6	45.2	28.9	3.3	19.4
1950	331.0	246.2	138.0	45.9	41.6	10.7	24.2
1951	427.4	287.3	153.1	64.2	67.0	17.3	14.9
1952	345.7	245.9	90.7	89.9	41.0	18.9	9.7
1953	398.3	292.9	117.0	95.8	38.9	28.9	15.7
1954	400.5	315.2	130.1	105.6	26.3	35.6	13.5
1955	400.6	314.5	118.7	106.3	27.8	41.5	12.8
1956	453.2	345.9	134.1	100.6	35.0	48.8	12.9
1957	431.1	322.7	132.0	82.8	39.0	45.1	15.1
1958	492.8	396.9	139.1	115.5	28.8	69.7	16.4
1959	529.5	420.9	138.1	112.6	38.9	80.4	18.2
1960	560.4	446.9	138.6	133.5	41.8	91.6	18.8
1961	499.5	396.2	88.2	135.1	28.8	92.4	14.5
1962	556.0	454.6	113.0	122.0	24.7	112.8	15.1
1963	727.1	609.1	168.3	146.5	31.6	152.9	18.4
1964	742.0	602.6	156.1	148.3	30.4	143.1	19.5
1965	768.5	637.6	170.0	132.4	24.2	162.0	20.4
1966	828.2	705.6	157.2	133.0	18.7	204.7	17.7
1967	821.5	673.9	129.4	141.7	14.7	212.2	17.0
1968	857.3	726.2	123.0	144.0	11.2	216.6	24.6
1969	854.6	709.0	87.3	148.8	14.3	226.0	16.1
1970	1,061.7	877.7	80.1	187.6	15.3	249.8	19.4
1971	1,121.8	928.2	114.0	212.3	c	225.9	20.7

Coconut Oil	Copra Meal or Cake	Pine-apples, Canned	Bananas	Veneer	Plywood	Copper Concen-trates
17.5	3.9	6.8	0	0.021	0.02	2.5
12.5	3.8	9.5	0	0.02	0.06	1.7
24.5	3.5	8.1	0		0.06	1.6
15.4	5.7	11.3	0	0.09	0.05	4.2
17.1	4.0	11.0	0	2.6	0.01	3.3
16.6	3.8	4.7	0	0.4	0.2	5.0
16.5	4.4	5.9	0	0.9	0.9	7.4
24.0	5.0	5.5	0	1.2	1.5	13.6
21.4	4.2	4.6	0	1.4	2.3	15.4
24.1	4.4	4.4	0	2.1	6.5	16.8
22.5	5.4	8.0	0	3.2	13.6	21.9
15.7	4.9	7.4	0.02	4.5	6.5	29.6
15.9	4.2	10.5	0.02	4.4	8.0	27.4
31.6	9.1	11.4	0	6.0	11.2	28.6
46.7	11.8	7.3	0	9.3	16.0	41.3
59.9	10.9	7.7	0.01	11.5	22.8	34.3
68.1	11.8	8.7	0	10.5	17.6	46.5
74.5	17.2	8.9	0.02	10.2	17.7	74.6
59.3	10.9	10.1	0.03	8.7	18.2	74.9
77.3	11.0	18.8	0	11.5	21.5	89.2
50.6	9.4	17.2	1.3	10.9	19.5	132.8
95.6	13.9	21.4	4.9	c	19.7	185.2
103.4	16.2	19.7	13.5	c	16.4	185.9

Source: Central Bank of the Philippines, *Annual Report* for various years.

a. The individual commodities listed include all those that were among the leading ten in 1969, 1970, and 1971.

b. This total consists of the ten leading commodities as of 1971.

c. No longer among the ten leading exports.

TABLE 1-4

International Transactions, 1946–71
(millions of U.S. dollars)

	1946–50	1951–55	1956–60	1961–65	1966–71
A. GOODS AND SERVICES					
Exports (f.o.b. incl. nonmonetary gold)	250.40	397.60	507.50	682.77	945.06
Imports	−504.82	−476.12	−561.10	−680.82	−1,080.45
Trade balance	−254.42	−78.52	−53.60	1.95	−135.39
Transportation and merchandise insurance	—	—	−60.58	−53.06	−76.95
Travel	—	—	−11.51	−23.32	17.29
Investment income	—	—	−58.47	−26.64	−86.22
Services rendered to U.S. military	241.18	143.12	25.34	24.89	59.52
Pensions from U.S. govt.	—	—	62.23	53.07	63.84
Private transfers	11.80	6.02	13.98	23.92	29.59
Other services	−77.88	−104.10	—	—	—
Other	—	—	9.58	63.15	26.76
Total A	−79.32	−33.48	−73.03	63.96	−101.20
B. OFFICIAL GRANTS AND LONG-TERM CAPITAL					
Reparations from Japan	—	—	20.74	12.21	32.53
Other official transfers	45.00	—	25.07	5.36	11.79
Private loans	—	7.34	10.24	2.02	73.68
Official loans	—	−1.36	5.38	20.82	23.43
Long-term foreign investment	20.20	28.20	26.93	−10.80	−4.78
Other official capital	5.50	−5.20	4.61	−0.20	−0.84
Total B	70.70	28.98	92.97	29.41	135.81
C. PRIVATE SHORT-TERM CAPITAL AND NET ERRORS AND OMISSIONS					
Private short-term capital	−18.82	−31.66	−0.40	−38.34	67.64
Net errors and omissions			−27.24	−83.58	−130.86
Total C	−18.82	−31.66	−27.64	−121.92	−63.22
D. ALLOCATION OF SPECIAL DRAWING RIGHTS	—	—	—	—	5.84
E. OVER-ALL POSITION (A + B + C + D)	−27.44	−36.16	−7.70	−28.55	−22.77

(continued)

TABLE 1–4 (*concluded*)

	1946–50	1951–55	1956–60	1961–65	1966–71
F. MONETARY MOVEMENTS					
Net IMF accounts	—	2.00	−1.58	0.36	15.70
Commercial bank liabilities			−2.08	36.92	15.19
Other central bank liabilities			5.74	21.87	36.79
Commercial bank assets[a]	52.20	39.56	−1.45	−3.15	−9.45
Central bank foreign exchange[a]			6.86	−9.02	−26.35
Central bank monetary gold[a]			0.13	−4.66	−4.80
Total F	52.20	41.56	7.62	42.32	27.08

SOURCE: Central Bank of the Philippines, *Annual Report*, various years.
a. Minus sign indicates increase.

TABLE 1-5

Distribution of Expenditures on Real Gross Domestic Product,[a] 1948–71
(percentage distribution)

	1948	1952	1955	1958	1961	1964	1967	1971
Personal consumption expenditures	84.0	84.0	87.7	83.8	81.9	78.6	74.6	72.8
General government expenditures	8.0	7.8	7.9	7.7	8.4	9.4	9.2	8.5
Gross domestic capital formation	19.0	11.0	12.3	13.6	15.2	17.5	17.3	19.5
Construction	12.6	8.1	7.2	7.8	8.0	8.4	8.2	5.4
Durable equipment	4.0	1.9	3.2	4.1	5.2	7.0	7.5	11.8
Change in stocks	2.4	1.0	1.9	1.7	2.0	2.1	1.6	2.3
Exports of goods and services	21.3	14.0	12.8	10.2	10.0	11.3	13.0	14.5
Less: Imports of goods and services	26.1	13.2	15.0	10.9	11.7	15.4	18.2	14.0
Expenditures on GDP	106.2	103.6	105.7	104.4	103.8	101.4	95.9	101.3

SOURCE: 1948–67—National Economic Council, *Statistical Reporter*, April–June 1969, p. 62; 1971—National Economic Council, "The Gross National Product and National Income of the Philippines, Calendar Year 1969 to Calendar Year 1971" (May 1972; mimeo.).
a. Prices for 1955 were used to deflate the figures in current prices for 1958 to 1967; 1967 prices were used to deflate 1971 current values.

average annual cash deficit of the national government between 1957 and 1970 was P51 million, an amount equal, however, to only about 2 per cent of average operating disbursements during this period.

PHASES OF EXCHANGE CONTROL IN THE PHILIPPINES

This section contains a brief survey of the payments policies pursued by the Philippine government between 1949 and 1971, presented in terms of the five phases of exchange control suggested by Bhagwati and Krueger (see Table 1-6).[10]

TABLE 1-6

Exchange-Control Phases in the Philippines, 1949–71

Dec. 1949–Sept. 1955	Phase I	Introduction and intensification of exchange controls
Sept. 1955–Apr. 1960	Phase II	Adoption of ad hoc measures to offset some of the unfavorable aspects of exchange controls
Apr. 1960–Jan. 1962	Phase III	Introduction of exchange-control liberalization
Jan. 1962–Nov. 1965	Phase IV	Continued liberalization of exchange controls
Nov. 1965–June 1967	Phase V	Period of complete liberalization
June 1967–Feb. 1970	Phase I	Return to moderate exchange controls
Feb. 1970–Dec. 1970	Phase III	Floating of peso and relaxation of some exchange controls
1971	Phase IV	Further relaxation of exchange controls

In Phase I, exchange controls are introduced, usually in response to an unsustainable balance-of-payments deficit, and gradually intensified. In the Philippines, exchange controls were first introduced in December 1949, after the government had experimented unsuccessfully earlier in the year with import quotas on luxury items. The immediate reason for the use of exchange controls was a full-scale foreign-exchange crisis near the end of 1949 that was closely associated with the expansionist monetary and fiscal policies pursued in connection with the presidential election in the fall of that year. More fundamentally, however, in the immediate postwar period the combination of pent-up demands for consumption and capital goods coupled with the reintroduction of the prewar peso-dollar exchange rate (P2 per dollar), despite a much increased relative cost structure, exerted considerable pressure on the trade balance. This pressure was initially contained by means of large-scale aid furnished by the United States. When this aid began to decline, in 1949, balance-of-payments problems quickly emerged.

Not only did exchange controls gradually intensify in the 1950s, but they became increasingly used to promote industrialization via import substitution. Industrialization became an important goal in the country immediately after the establishment of Philippine independence in 1946. However, although special tax exemptions were granted "new and necessary" industries as early as 1946, it was not until import and exchange controls were introduced that significant progress beyond restoring prewar manufacturing was made in substituting domestic manufacturing for imports of manufactures. Imports of consumption goods under the exchange-control system were, for example, reduced from 50 per cent of total imports in 1950 to less than 15 per cent by 1960. Thus, although exchange control was not deliberately introduced for the purpose of fostering import substitution, this goal soon served as the main rationale for continuing controls over foreign-exchange transactions.

In Phase II policymakers begin to perceive such undesirable effects of comprehensive exchange controls as the disincentive effect on exporters and the reaping of large windfall gains by importers. Consequently, the government adopts various ad hoc measures to combat these effects. It is not possible accurately to date the beginning of Phase II in the Philippines. To a growing degree, as the 1950s progressed, there was dissatisfaction with the system and a realization that there were serious drawbacks associated with it. The main attempt to offset part of the penalty imposed on exporters by the overvalued exchange rate was the enactment, in September 1955, of a law permitting a limited amount of export goods to be bartered for imports outside of the exchange-control system. Efforts to obtain part of the windfall gains related to exchange controls occurred as early as 1950 with an increase in the sales tax and in 1951 with the imposition of a 17 per cent excise tax on the peso price of foreign exchange sold by the banking system. The rise in tariff rates under the Laurel-Langley Agreement in 1955 was also partly directed at capturing windfall gains.[11]

Phase III in the Bhagwati-Krueger schema, the period when formal liberalization efforts are initiated, began in the Philippines in early 1960 when the Central Bank introduced a multiple exchange-rate system. Except for gold sales and tourist receipts as well as purchases of essential goods and certain services, all transactions took place at rates higher than the traditional figure of P2 per dollar. This exchange depreciation was considered to be a first step in a gradual and orderly liberalization process that was to extend over three or four years. It was followed, in the fall of 1960 and spring of 1961, by further increases in foreign-exchange sales by the Central Bank at the depreciated rate (P3.2 and then P3.0 per dollar).

With the inauguration of a new president, in 1962, the plan for gradual liberalization was scrapped in favor of almost complete decontrol and a temporary (until June) floating of the exchange rate. This marked the beginning of Phase IV in the Bhagwati-Krueger schema of exchange regimes, namely, a period of continued liberalization. The decontrol effort fell short of complete liberalization because of the introduction of special time-deposit requirements for letters of credit (in place of the levy on foreign exchange, which was abolished) and a requirement that 20 per cent of export receipts be surrendered at the old exchange rate of P2 per dollar. The time-deposit requirement was gradually liberalized in 1963 and 1964, but the penalty rate for exporters was not removed until a unified rate of P3.90 per dollar was established in 1965.

From late 1965 until mid-1967 the Philippine economy was free of all forms of exchange control and thus could be characterized as being in the final stage of the Bhagwati-Krueger schema, namely, Phase V. The period of complete liberalization was comparatively short-lived, however. Balance-of-payments problems due to the high import level stimulated by the government's easy credit policies and expanded development-oriented expenditure programs were held off for a few years by extensive foreign borrowing from official and private sources. However, as the limited nature of these resources became obvious, the Central Bank reintroduced time-deposit requirements for various classes of imports in June 1967. A steady worsening of the balance-of-payments situation in 1968 and especially in 1969 led to a rise in these requirements in 1968, and finally, in 1969, to the banning of certain nonessential imports. Thus, in 1967 the Philippines could be characterized as re-entering Phase I of the exchange-control schema, though the controls were moderate compared to those of the early 1950s.

When a severe exchange crisis developed, in late 1969 and early 1970, the government elected, in February of 1970, to float the peso and simultaneously eliminate many of the exchange controls that had been introduced since 1967 rather than hold to the existing exchange rate and adopt much more stringent exchange controls. In other words, the government adopted the kind of liberalization policies that typify Phase III in the outline of exchange-control stages. As with the 1962 currency depreciation, exporters were not permitted to exchange all of their dollar earnings at the market rate. Instead, it was required that 80 per cent of the receipts from the major export products be exchanged at the old rate of P3.90 per dollar. This discriminatory treatment of exporters was, however, soon replaced, in May 1970, by an arrangement that permitted exporters to sell their foreign exchange at the free rate but required them to pay a tax on the value of their exports ranging from 8 to 10 per cent. The exchange rate was eventually fixed, in December 1970, at P6.4 per dollar. Gradual movement during 1971 toward further liberalization meant that the economy could be said to be in Phase IV of the exchange-control schema. However, as of early 1972, a prior-deposit requirement still existed, the importation of certain items still could be made only with permission of the Central Bank, and the export tax still was in effect. The exchange rate was also permitted to rise again, in April of 1972, to P6.7 per dollar.

In the next two chapters, a much more detailed description will be given of the various trade and payments policies as well as the related monetary and fiscal measures that were used in the Philippines during the various exchange-control phases of the Bhagwati-Krueger outline. One of the justifications for the series of country studies of which this is a part is that, in order to make further progress in understanding the reasons for the success or failure of various foreign-trade regimes, it is necessary to examine in detail the nature of these regimes in several countries. In short, one must get down to the "nitty gritty" of exchange-control and commercial policies in different economic environments in order to discover why these policies succeed in some circumstances and fail in others. One of the benefits of this approach is that it indicates how a whole series of domestic and international policies are used in an interrelated manner to achieve a goal such as industrialization. To understand the protection afforded to import-competing industries in the Philippines, for example, an investigation limited to exchange-rate and tariff policies is not enough. Such measures as discriminatory sales taxes, margin-deposit requirements, tax exemptions, subsidized lending, and special foreign-exchange fees have been important complements of these policies.

Still another advantage of attention to detail is that it brings out how varied and rapidly changing has been intervention by the Philippine government in the trade and payments field. Economic policy in most countries is not run as if some superhuman mind clearly perceived the economic objectives to be pursued or how any particular measure would affect the achievement of these goals. Instead, there are often elements of both contradiction and overkill in the several policies employed in attempting to reach a particular goal. Moreover, when new groups achieve governmental power or old ones gain experience, the package of economic policies often changes significantly.

A drawback of an in-depth description of external and internal economic policies is that one may be unable to see the forest for the trees. In order to help overcome this problem, brief outlines of the major measures adopted in a particular period will be presented in Chapters 2, 3, and 4 as well as occasional summaries of the main trends. In addition, in Chapter 5, quantitative estimates over time of the combined protective effect of the various policies reported in Chapters 2, 3, and 4 will be presented. Included in an appendix to Chapter 5, for example, are quantitative estimates of the relative importance of the different measures employed to encourage industrialization. The main purpose of the detailed presentation in Chapters 2 through 4 is, therefore, to convey to the reader an appreciation of the complexity and changeability of Philippine economic policies as well as an understanding of the techniques employed to achieve (often conflicting) economic goals.

NOTES

1. Southeast Asia is generally defined as being composed of the following nine countries: Burma, Thailand, South Vietnam, Laos, Cambodia, Malaysia, Singapore, Indonesia, and the Philippines.

2. An average exchange rate for 1970 of P5.895 per dollar is used in this calculation.

3. United Nations, Department of Economics and Social Affairs, *Statistical Yearbook, 1971* (New York, 1972).

4. Ibid., *1970*, p. 712.

5. Frank H. Golay, *The Philippines: Public Policy and National Economic Development* (Ithaca: Cornell University Press, 1961), p. 294.

6. Ibid., p. 300.

7. United Nations, Economic Commission for Asia and the Far East, *Statistical Yearbook for Asia and the Far East, 1971* (Bangkok, 1972).

8. Income from government property added another 4 per cent.

9. International Monetary Fund, *International Financial Statistics,* December 1970 and December 1971.

10. See Appendix A for a detailed description of the phases.

11. The Laurel-Langley Agreement, or the Revised Trade Agreement as it is officially called, is a modification of the U.S.-Philippine Trade Act (the Bell Trade Act) of 1946, which stipulated the manner in which free trade between the two countries would gradually end. The Laurel-Langley Agreement raised the Philippine tariff level and accelerated the pace at which imports from the United States would be subject to the full Philippine tariff rates.

Chapter 2

Exchange Controls and Related Development Policies, 1946-59

1946-49: THE RECONSTRUCTION PERIOD

The main economic goals of the Philippine government in the immediate postwar years were to restore prewar production levels, initiate an industrialization effort, and ensure adequate supplies of essential consumption and capital goods. Table 2-1 contains a summary of the main trade, fiscal, and monetary measures directed at these objectives.

Reducing Imports of Consumption Goods.

World War II resulted in severe devastation of the Philippine economy. As Paul McNutt (the last high commissioner from the United States) reported, at the end of the war only a bare remnant of the major industrial equipment was intact; not a single sugar mill was operating; the fishing fleets has been taken away or destroyed; rolling stock had been carried away to Japan; and mile after mile of concrete highway had been destroyed.[1] In 1946, the first year of the reconstruction period, total output was only 35 per cent of its 1940 level. The mining and manufacturing sectors were especially hard hit by the war, and 1946 production levels in those sectors were only 1 and 18 per cent, respectively, of their 1940 levels.[2]

Fortunately, large disbursements by the U.S. government in the form of war damage payments, relief expenditures, veterans' pensions, and military expenditures, as well as a remarkably rapid expansion of export proceeds permitted the country to ease the shortage of domestically produced goods

17

TABLE 2-1

Major Trade, Payments, and Related Economic Policies, 1946–49

July 1946	United States–Philippines Trade Agreement providing for eight-year free-trade period between the countries and restricting Philippines' ability to change its exchange rate or impose exchange controls
Sept. 1946	Exemptions from domestic taxes for "new and necessary" industries
Oct. 1946	Establishment of Rehabilitation Finance Corporation to provide low-cost loans for reconstruction and development
June 1948	Increase in the sales tax on luxury and semiluxury items (most of which were imported) from 20 to 30 per cent and from 10 to 15 per cent, respectively
July 1948	Enactment of Import Control Act, leading to imposition of import quotas on nonessential and luxury imports
Nov. 1949	Imposition by Central Bank of 80 per cent margin requirement on all letters of credit covering imports of luxury and nonessential goods
Dec. 1949	Institution of foreign-exchange controls by Central Bank
	Increase by Central Bank in annual rediscount rate from 1.5 per cent to 3 per cent

with substantial imports. For the two years 1945 and 1946, for example, total U.S. government expenditures of $393 million more than covered combined imports of $364 million.[3] Thereafter, the rapid rise in exports, from $64 million in 1946 to $327 million in 1948, coupled with continued high levels of U.S. government expenditures and foreign aid resulted in a rise of imports to an average of $613 million between 1947 and 1949—an average level that was then one-third larger than the prewar value and was not again reached until the early 1960s. The outstanding export performance was due in large part to a rapid increase in export prices. The index of these prices (1937 = 100) rose from 156 in 1946 to 291 in 1948. The volume of exports in 1948 was still only 74 per cent of the 1937 level.

Policymakers were, however, concerned at the time by the high consumption component of imports. In 1947, consumption goods made up 68 per cent of all imports (one-quarter of these were textiles), and capital goods averaged about 10 per cent of imports. Although the share of capital goods was not too different from the 14 per cent figure of 1937–40, top government officials believed that this level was insufficient to meet the country's reconstruction and development requirements. Most Philippine leaders believed that the country needed both additional export-oriented and import-replacing production in order to meet the adjustment problem associated with the gradual phasing out of reciprocal preferential relations with the United States.[4] Achieving these increases in production in turn required additional imports of capital equipment. The concern of government authorities was further heightened by the steady depletion of the international reserves which had been built up in 1945 from large U.S. government expenditures.

The policy options available to the Philippine government to achieve its import-substitution goals and meet the growing deficit problem were severely constrained by the provisions of the Philippine Trade Act of 1946 (the Bell Trade Act). This act, passed by the U.S. Congress shortly before the scheduled independence date for the Philippines (July 4, 1946), and accepted by the Philippines as of that date as an Executive Trade Agreement between the United States and the Philippines, provided for an eight-year period (until July 1954) of free trade between the two countries. For the rest of 1954 each country was to tax imports at 5 per cent of its full rate. Beginning in 1955, the tariff on imports was to be at 10 per cent of the full rate. Thereafter, this level was to be raised by five percentage points per year until full duties would apply as of January 1973.[5] The act also stipulated that until 1973 the Philippine government could not change the established exchange rate of 2 pesos per U.S. dollar, impose exchange inconvertibility, or restrict capital transfers without explicit agreement from the President of the United States.[6] Since the United States supplied 80 per cent of Philippine imports in this period, the effect of the free-trade agreement between the countries was to rule out tariff increases as a means of reducing imports. Likewise it was evident that permission to devalue the currency or impose exchange control was likely to be given by the United States only if a severe exchange crisis developed. Two other features of the act that infringed upon Philippine sovereignty were the commitment not to levy export taxes and the agreement to accord Americans equal rights with Filipinos in the exploitation and development of natural resources and public utilities in the Philippines. As Golay remarks, the act was accepted by the Filipinos because it was accompanied by another piece of legislation providing for U.S. compensation for war damages suffered in the country.[7]

Despite the constraints imposed by the Bell Act, it was not long before the government found means other than tariffs to restrain imports. One method, adopted in June of 1948, was to raise the sales tax on luxury and semiluxury items—most of which were imported—from 20 to 30 per cent and from 10 to 15 per cent, respectively. The measure also stipulated that the sales tax be paid in advance on imported articles, i.e., prior to their release by customs officials. More important as a means of limiting imports, however, was enactment of the Import Control Act (Republic Act [R.A.] No. 330) in July of the same year. Under this law, which was not considered to be inconsistent with the Bell Trade Act, but was not implemented until January 1949 because of the opposition of foreign importers, President Elpidio Quirino was authorized to establish a system of import control by regulating imports of nonessential and luxury articles and to create an Import Control Board to devise the necessary rules and regulations. The intent of the act was not so much to encourage the domestic production of nonessential items, but, by restricting imports of luxury goods, to permit the importation of a sufficient volume of essential consumer goods for lower-income groups and of essential capital goods for basic reconstruction and development needs.[8]

The mechanics of import restriction under the Import Control Act involved placing various imports on a list of so-called luxury or nonessential items and then requiring import licensing for these goods by the three-man board set up under the act.[9] To begin operation of the controls, the value of imports from July 1, 1947, to July 30, 1948 was established as the base period; and then (as of January 1949) current imports were permitted equal in value terms to between 5 and 80 per cent of these base-period imports. Imports of commodities that were produced locally were given the greatest percentage cuts. A definite share of imports was reserved for new importers, first, without any nationality requirement, but then later only for Filipinos. Another feature of the control system aimed at curtailing primarily luxury goods was that import quotas for some categories of goods applied only if the c.i.f. unit values of the items were high enough to make them among the most expensive types of a particular class of goods.

Introduction of Exchange Controls.

Despite increases both in the range of items brought under control and in the percentage cutbacks during the second half of the year, the volume of imports actually was slightly larger in 1949 than in 1948. Only imports of tobacco products declined significantly. There was also no significant change in the commodity distribution of imports.[10]

One reason for this failure was a shifting from high-priced to low-priced imports of a particular commodity. Import controls applied, for example, only to automobiles costing more than $3,500. By purchasing mainly inexpensive cars, importers were able to increase the value of imported cars from $7 million to $8 million in the first half of 1949. Permitting importers to transfer quotas among articles also operated to frustrate any pattern of differential cutbacks. More fundamentally, however, the poor performance in cutting imports was due to an unwillingness of the government to impose the harsh monetary and fiscal measures needed. The year 1949 was a presidential election year, and one can observe at this early date the pattern of deficit spending, increases in the money supply, and a tendency to ease controls that characterizes election years up to the present time.[11] For example, the government deficit from July 1, 1949, to June 30, 1950 (elections are in November), was $212 million compared to levels in the $50 million–$70 million range before and after the election. Obviously, this deficit spending added to the pressure for large imports. The governor of the Central Bank warned President Quirino in early 1949 that, due to rapidly increasing imports, exchange control would have to be imposed by the end of the year unless appropriate alternative measures were taken. However, according to the governor, no action was taken because it was an election year.[12] Apparently, political pressures were effective in thwarting the implementation of the Import Control Act in that year.[13]

The failure to reduce imports in 1949 probably would not have resulted in the full-scale exchange crisis which developed near the end of the year had it not been accompanied by a sharp drop in both exports and U.S. government expenditures. The value of exports dropped from $327 million in 1948 to $261 million in 1949, even though the volume rose somewhat. The reason for the decline in value was a sharp drop in the prices of coconut products, the product group that made up 68 per cent of the country's exports in the 1947–49 period. Still another factor precipitating the crisis was a capital flight near the end of 1949 based on the fear that the Philippines would fall in line with the devaluation pattern followed by a number of countries in September of that year.[14]

The drop in international reserves from $420 million in 1948 to $260 million in 1949 led the Central Bank, which had only opened for business on January 3, 1949, to intervene in the exchange market immediately after the election. First, on November 17, the bank issued Circular 19, under which an 80 per cent margin requirement was imposed on all letters of credit covering various luxury and nonessential items. The list of items was substantially the same as the one that formed the basis for the initial implementation of the Import Control Act. Commercial banks were also prohibited from granting credit facilities either directly or indirectly for the purpose of providing the margin requirements. Next, on December 9, 1949, the Central Bank instituted foreign-exchange controls by issuing Circular 20 under the authority vested in the bank by the act (R.A. 265) that had established it. Before doing so, however, the consent of the President of the United States was obtained, as required by the Philippine Trade Act of 1946. The circular stipulated that all transactions in gold and foreign exchange must be licensed by the Central Bank and all receipts of foreign exchange must be sold to the Bank. On December 29, the Central Bank also raised its rediscount rate from the very low rate of 1.5 per cent to 3.0 per cent.[15]

Thus, the immediate reason for the imposition of exchange controls was an exchange crisis touched off by liberal spending and credit policies related to the 1949 election. However, more basic reasons for the underlying weakness in the country's balance-of-payments conditions were pent-up demand for both consumption and capital goods coupled with an unrealistically low price for foreign exchange.

Tax Exemption and Special Financing Facilities.

Although the promotion of domestic industrial development does not appear to have been the main purpose of the early import controls, the government, soon after gaining its independence, did utilize special tax and financing privileges for the specific purpose of fostering "new and necessary" industries. The enabling act (R.A. 35, September 1946) exempted new industries from all internal (but not import) taxes for a period of four years from the time the industry was organized. While "new and necessary" industries were not defined in the act, the Secretary of Finance in an implementing order specified these industries to be ones that "had not been commercially exploited in the Philippines before the war" and that "contribute to industrial and economic development." The latter phrase was regarded by the Finance Secretary as being general enough to cover a very wide variety of manufacturing activities. However, despite this broad interpretation and even though aliens as well as Filipinos could enjoy the tax benefits, only one new manufacturing corporation availed itself of the tax exemption as of March 1948.[16] It was not until import controls were introduced, in 1949, that the number of firms applying for the privilege became significant. This poor response to tax incentives seems to have been due to the absence of tariffs on imports of manufactures from the United States coupled with an abundance of U.S. aid and the profitability of reconstructing previously established industries.[17]

Another governmental measure that should be mentioned as contributing to the import-substitution efforts initiated in the reconstruction period was the 1946 act establishing the Rehabilitation Finance Corporation (RFC). This organization, with an initial authorized capital of P300 million and lending rates below those in the free market, became the major source of industrial credit in the economy. In the 1947–49 period the RFC approved loans averaging about $45 million annually. Real estate construction and repair absorbed 51 per cent of this sum (a share that rapidly decreased as war-damaged buildings were repaired or replaced); the industrial sector, 28 per cent; and agricultural activities and the government, the remaining 21 per cent.

1950–52: THE EARLY YEARS
OF EXCHANGE CONTROL

The exchange-control experience of the first few years of the 1950s is noteworthy for two main reasons. First, after exchange controls were introduced by the Central Bank, in December 1949, government controls rapidly spread to all types of international transactions and became increasingly complex. Second, prices of imported goods increased sharply, in part because of the Korean War, but mainly because of the restrictive import controls. The government responded to the price increases by adopting tax measures designed to capture the windfall gains associated with exchange controls and also by liberalizing import controls over the more essential consumer goods and raw materials. As is shown in the statistical analysis of Chapter 5, it was during this period that the pattern—so typical in many developing nations—was firmly established of protecting commodities generally classified as luxury items compared to capital goods, essential raw materials, and basic consumption goods. Table 2-2 summarizes the main policy changes in the 1950–52 period.

The Nature of Import and Exchange Controls.

Republic Act 426, passed in May 1950, illustrates the growing complexity of import controls. This law stipulated that import licenses issued by the Import Control Board be required for all articles imported into the country. These imports were divided into four groups, depending upon their degree of essentiality; and maximum and minimum percentage cuts from 1946–48 trade levels were established for each group. The first category, prime imports, consisted of items regarded as being of prime necessity and as not being in sufficient supply locally.[18] Quotas established for these goods were to reduce the value of imports in the base period by no more than 40 per cent. The second group, essential imports, consisted of articles that were regarded as necessary (but not of prime necessity) for the health and well-being of the people. Imports of these items were to be cut back so as to encourage their domestic production.[19] The legislated reduction on these imports was to be no less than 40 per cent nor more than 60 per cent. Nonessential imports, the third category, were defined as items "not necessary for the health and material well-being of the people, but whose consumption is concomitant with the rise of their standard of living." [20] These were to be cut between 60 and 80 per cent to encourage their domestic production in sufficient quantities to meet local demand. Luxury imports, the last group, were categorized as articles primarily "for ostentation or pleasure" and were to be reduced between 80 and 90 per cent.[21] The main items specifically not subject to import quota allocation under the law were raw materials used in the manufacture of goods on the list of so-called prime imports, supplies and equipment for the Philippine government, and books and supplies for schools and charitable organizations. Moreover, agricultural equipment and "other machinery, materials, and equipment for dollar-producing, and dollar-saving industries" were excluded from

TABLE 2-2

Major Trade, Payments, and Related Economic Policies, 1950–52

May 1950	New Import Control Act requiring import licenses for all imports, stressing the import-substitution objective, and giving preference to Filipino citizens
June 1950	Price controls instituted, covering essential consumer goods, raw materials, and machinery
Sept. 1950	Increases in sales taxes, with greatest rise occurring in luxury consumer items
Dec. 1950	Issuance of Executive Order permitting certain highly essential consumer goods and raw materials to be imported without quota limitations in order to hold prices down
Feb. 1951	Increases in base on which sales tax calculation is made for imported goods; again, greatest increase occurred for luxury consumer goods
Mar. 1951	Imposition of 17 per cent excise tax on peso value of foreign exchange sold by banking system
May 1951	Adoption of still another Import Control Act completely decontrolling a number of essential consumer items but also extending import-substitution goal by stating as an objective that nonessential commodity imports be reduced or banned; re-export of certain essential goods also banned
June 1951	Further easing through an Executive Order of the importation of additional essential commodities in order to stem increase in domestic prices
Aug. 1951	Retrenchment of liberalization policy by reducing number of decontrolled items and establishing list of banned items
May 1952	Introduction of measures designed to make it more difficult to undervalue exports
Aug. 1952	Reduction of rediscount rate from 3 per cent to 2 per cent

the provision that items not enumerated in the control lists (about 55 per cent of 1949 imports) would not be granted import licenses that resulted in imports exceeding their 1948 levels.

The import-substituting objective was stated much more clearly in the 1950 act than in the Import Control Act of 1948. If the domestic production of a commodity was deemed sufficient to meet local demand by the secretaries of Agriculture and Commerce, the Import Control Board was required to impose the maximum percentage cut stipulated for the appropriate category to which the item belonged. In addition to that, an uncontrolled item could be moved into the list of controlled goods and a controlled item could be moved to a more restrictive category.

We can see quite clearly at this early stage how the Philippines embarked upon an industrialization policy directed not only at import-substitution activities rather than export-promoting ones but also at the production of many nonessential consumption commodities. Instead of attempting to remove exchange controls once the 1949 crisis had passed, policymakers decided to continue to employ these controls to carry out their export-promoting and import-replacing goals. With a simplistic view of economic interrelationships, these leaders reasoned that the capital goods needed for an expansion of export-oriented and basic import-replacing production would be more or less automatically imported once imports of consumption goods were forcibly curtailed. They also concluded that the most plausible criterion for restricting these consumption imports was their degree of essentiality in terms of basic nutritional and health needs. Thus, imports of so-called luxury items were sharply curtailed. They had overlooked the tendency of capital to flow into the most profitable industries and that the act of restricting imports of nonessential consumption goods would raise the domestic prices of these goods sharply and thereby make their production the most profitable opportunity available. Imports of luxury goods were restricted so severely that the production incentives brought about by this act dominated all the other policies aimed at encouraging the manufacturing sector.

Another important feature of the 1950 Import Control Act was the marked preference it gave to Filipino citizens. The Import Control Board was instructed to reserve 30 per cent of the total import quota for any article in the fiscal year 1950–51, 40 per cent in 1951–52, and 50 per cent in 1952–53 to new Filipino importers. At least 60 per cent of a company's stock had to be owned by Filipinos for a firm to qualify under this provision of the law. Existing import businesses, which had long been dominated by Westerners and Chinese, received the remaining quota allocations.[22]

The granting of an import license by the Import Control Board automatically entitled an importer to a foreign-exchange license. However, the Monetary Board, which supervised exchange control, informed the Control Board from time to time (apparently every six months) of the amount of foreign exchange available for any specified period for imports. Import licenses were not to be issued in amounts that would exceed the available foreign-exchange supply.

Besides cutting down on commodity imports, the Central Bank modestly curtailed the amount of foreign exchange available for service transactions.[23]

Controls were also imposed on the remittance of earnings of foreign companies. Initially, the amount of income transferable could represent 10 per cent of the foreign participation in the current net profits or capital stock as of December 31, 1949, whichever was higher. In order to attract foreign capital, this provision was relaxed, in May 1950, to permit the additional remittance of earnings representing 30 per cent of the foreign participation in either the fixed assets or capital stock of the company, whichever was higher.

The efforts of the Central Bank and Import Control Board to conserve foreign exchange proved very successful, and imports declined 20 per cent between 1949 and 1950. Furthermore, in line with the import-substitution policy that began in earnest in 1950, the composition of imports shifted significantly from consumption goods to raw materials and capital goods. Consumption goods constituted 64 per cent of total imports in 1949 but only 50 per cent in 1950. As the analysis in Chapter 5 indicates, implicit protective rates of 200 per cent or more for nonessential consumer goods were not unusual in this period. The share of raw materials imports increased from 26 to 38 per cent, and that of capital goods, from 10 to 12 per cent between the two years. The success of the policy in actually stimulating domestic production is indicated by the sharp rise in the net capital of firms granted tax exemptions —from P2.7 million in 1949 to P8.6 million in 1950.[24] The shift was also aided by the moral suasion exerted on commercial banks by the Central Bank to limit real estate and consumption loans and direct more of their credit operations to production.

Not only did imports drop in 1950, but starting in August exports rose sharply due to increases in demand related to the Korean War. During the year export prices rose 12 per cent, and the value of exports, 30 per cent. Consequently, the current account balance shifted from a $68 million deficit in 1949 to a $189 million surplus in 1950, while reserves rose by $96 million.

Controlling Price Increases and Windfall Gains.

A significant consequence of the tight import controls instituted in 1950 was upward pressure on the domestic prices of imported goods. These prices rose 21 per cent from 1949 to 1950. To offset this pressure a price control bill (R.A. 509) was passed, in June 1950, which was intended "to prevent, locally or generally, scarcity, monopolization, and profiteering, from affecting the supply . . . of both imported and locally manufactured" goods for which price control was deemed in the public interest. The group of commodities covered reflected the government's concern for maintaining low prices for basic consumer goods, machinery, and certain raw materials. Specifically, the categories covered by price controls were stipulated to be manufactured foodstuffs, textiles, clothing, paper, school supplies, building materials, agricultural and industrial machinery, and fuel and lubricants.

In still another attempt to hold prices down, President Quirino issued Executive Order 388, in late December 1950, stipulating that certain "prime commodities and raw materials in short supply in the Philippines" be imported without quota allocation during the first quarter of 1951. In a new import act, in May of 1951 (R.A. 650), these efforts were supplemented by the establishment of a class of "completely decontrolled items" which included the items mentioned in previous executive orders and to which were added a few more consumption articles. A second specified category, "essential items of import," consisted mainly of a long list of manufactured intermediate commodities and capital goods. In budgeting for essential imports the administering authorities were instructed to give priority to imports of machinery and raw materials for essential industries and to the needs of government agencies engaged in stockpiling essential goods and in stabilizing prices. Second priority was to be granted to the equipment and raw materials requirements of bona fide producers of nonessentials to the extent that these requirements could not be adequately met from local supplies. The balance of foreign exchange available after meeting the first two priorities was distributed to businesses and bona fide importers in proportion to their 1949 import levels, including a reasonable allocation for new Filipino importers. No specific list of nonessentials was appended to the act, but it was stated that an objective should be to reduce or ban the importation of these latter types of commodities.

Two other anti-inflationary measures taken by the government in May 1951 were: (1) a lifting of the 80 per cent margin requirement introduced in 1949 for certain textile imports that had become important raw materials for the industry, and (2) the banning of re-exports of such goods as machines, medicines, foodstuffs, oils and gasoline, and scrap metals (R.A. 613). On the other hand, one conspicuously absent anti-inflationary policy was a tight monetary policy.[25] The money supply had expanded 19 per cent between 1949 and 1950, and in early 1951 credit still remained easy.[26]

These efforts to restrain the upward movement of prices were not very successful until the latter part of 1951, as the retail price indices for selected commodities shown in Table 2-3 indicate.[27] With regard to the late 1950 and 1951 period, it is noted in the Central Bank *Annual Report* that "the expanded purchasing power due to inflated export earnings, heavy final war damage payments, and deficit financing was being penned in by the stringent import and exchange controls in force and was pushing prices up."[28] A rough notion of the profitability in producing import-competing goods domestically is indicated by the fact that, although the c.i.f. unit value of imported goods in 1951 actually was less than in 1949, wholesale prices of imported goods in 1951 were 53 per cent above their 1949 level. Wholesale prices of locally produced goods for home consumption rose less than 1 per cent between 1949 and 1951. This protective effect of import controls is analyzed in detail in Chapter 5.

TABLE 2-3

Retail Prices of Selected Commodities, 1950–51
(January 1950 = 100)

	July 1950	Jan. 1951	July 1951	Dec. 1951
All items	102.7	113.0	122.2	117.2
Foodstuff	99.7	113.3	111.6	110.3
Wearing apparel	99.4	120.3	135.6	112.5
Construction materials	101.0	105.3	126.6	117.7
Fuel	106.5	103.8	110.6	110.6
Drugs and medicine	100.3	122.3	124.7	115.8
School supplies	117.0	102.6	155.4	142.1
Cigarettes and cigars	129.1	127.8	140.2	116.5
Liquor	108.8	119.7	151.2	121.4
Kitchen utensils	108.7	150.6	182.0	178.6
Starch and oils	124.5	148.7	141.0	143.0
Soap	92.3	113.1	97.7	92.3
Electrical supplies	103.2	99.2	167.5	215.8

SOURCE: Central Bank of the Philippines, *Annual Report*, 1951, pp. 181–182.

The government was, however, successful in capturing some of the wind-fall gains going to many importers. First, in September 1950, the sales tax on both imported and domestically produced goods was raised. For jewelry, medium-priced automobiles, and toilet preparations, the rate was raised from 30 per cent to 50 per cent (to 75 per cent in the case of high-priced automobiles); for lower-priced automobiles, sporting goods, refrigerators, radios, phonographs, washing machines, firearms, etc., from 15 to 30 per cent; and for all other articles, from 5 to 7 per cent. Next, in February 1951, the base for calculating the sales tax on imported goods was increased to 200 per cent of the c.i.f. value for the first group of items, 150 per cent for the second, and 125 per cent for all other imports. As the analysis in Chapter 5 indicates, in the absence of these measures windfall gains of 100 percent or more would have been obtained in 1951 from selling many imported nonessential goods. A noteworthy point about this discriminatory customs valuation measure is that, when exchange controls and such measures as special trade taxes and margin requirements were finally lifted, in the 1960s, this measure remained in effect and, together with the tariff structure, still provided a high degree of protection to domestic industries producing nonessential consumer goods.

Besides raising the sales tax, the government in the fall of 1950 increased the rate of taxation on personal and corporate income. The rate on corporate income, for example, was increased from 12 per cent to 16 per cent. In 1951 the corporate rate was again raised so that the tax level on incomes below P100,000 became 20 per cent. Direct taxes, however, still remained a relatively unimportant source of government tax revenue. Their 1950 share of total tax revenue was only about 17 per cent.

These actions were followed, in late March 1951, by the imposition of a 17 per cent excise tax on the peso value of foreign exchange sold by the Central Bank or commercial banks (R.A. 601). This measure had been recommended, mainly for the purpose of raising revenue and reducing imports, by the Bell Mission, an economic survey group sent from the United States, at President Quirino's request.[29] However, because domestic prices were already considerably above c.i.f. prices for tightly controlled items, the tax had the apparent initial effect of capturing windfall gains rather than cutting imports.[30] Upward price pressure on essential items subject to a liberal control policy was prevented by forgoing or refunding the tax on such items.[31] Furthermore, the tax was not levied at all on foreign exchange used to purchase machines and raw materials by the "new and necessary" industries covered by R.A. 35.[32]

In June 1951 the President further expanded the list of items exempted from quota allocation in order "to arrest the rising trend of prices and discourage speculation." Under Executive Order 446 the Price Stabilization Corporation was authorized to import some 150 specifically mentioned items "in such quantities as may be found necessary." The list included not only basic consumer goods but the main raw materials and capital goods used by the industrial and agricultural sectors.

The policy of attempting to hold down prices by liberalizing the country's import policy began to conflict with the objective of stimulating import-substituting production through protection. It was claimed, for example, that the easing of controls led to excessive stockpiling and a glut of certain imported goods to the detriment of local production.[33] Consequently, in August 1951, the President instituted a retrenchment in his liberalization policy (Executive Order 471). As already noted, the import legislation passed in May had directed the control authorities to "reduce or ban" both nonessentials and commodities produced "economically and in sufficient quantities" domestically, but Executive Order 471 went a step further in actually setting out a schedule for banning such imports. Almost 150 items were to be banned immediately and another 20 by July 1952. The number of completely decontrolled items was also reduced from 19 to 6. Nevertheless, the government did succeed in halting the rise in the retail prices of imported goods. As is indicated in Table 2-3, the index of retail prices fell from a high of 122 in July 1951 (January 1950 = 100) to 117 in December 1951. The money supply actually declined 5 per cent during the year as the government fought the inflation by liberalizing imports. However, the balance-of-trade deficit rose from $5 million in 1950 to $76 million in 1951.

No significant changes in economic policy occurred in 1952. Although some steps were taken to make it more difficult to undervalue exports, imports continued to be closely regulated by means of import and exchange controls, while such measures as the 80 per cent margin requirement on letters of credit for the importation of specified luxury and nonessential items and the 17 per cent tax on foreign exchange further discouraged imports. However, the Central Bank did lower the rediscount rate from 3 per cent to 2 per cent in August 1952. Retail prices continued the decline begun in mid-1951, and the trade account deficit remained at about its 1951 level.

1953–59: FURTHER EFFORTS TO PROMOTE IMPORT SUBSTITUTION

The year 1953 is an important one in any survey of Philippine experience with trade controls because the Congress, in response to continued charges of favoritism and excessive delays on the part of the authorities administering import controls,[34] failed to extend the Import Control Act when it expired in June of that year. The Executive branch responded by placing the entire control mechanism in the hands of the Central Bank. This shift reduced the number of charges of favoritism and excess delays in the allocation of foreign exchange but did not change the general goal of import substitution. This objective was vigorously pursued by the Central Bank and other agencies throughout the rest of the 1950s. By 1959 protective rates of 400 per cent or more were not uncommon in the category of nonessential consumer goods. Besides holding to the belief that exchange controls were helpful in fostering industrialization and to the policy of providing low-priced essential consumer goods for lower-income groups, Central Bank authorities found exchange controls desirable from the viewpoint of their responsibilities "to maintain monetary stability" and "to preserve the international value of the peso." Fear of inflation and a resulting exchange crisis and depreciation should controls be removed was frequently expressed by these authorities during the 1950s. However, there were growing pressures from exporters to be permitted to trade at a more favorable exchange rate. They pointed out that the overvaluation of the peso acted to discourage production for export purposes. Finally, in 1955 a "no-dollar import law" was passed that enabled certain exports to be bartered for imports outside of the exchange system.[35] Largely because of this law, the second phase of the Bhagwati-Krueger schema, namely, the adoption of ad hoc measures to offset some of the unfavorable aspects of exchange control, is dated as beginning in 1955.

In this section, trade and related policies during the entire 1953–59 period are described in five broad areas of special interest: operation of exchange controls by the Central Bank; monetary and fiscal measures; changes in tariffs; tax exemptions for new firms; and finally, measures designed to increase exports. Table 2-4 contains summaries of the major trade-related measures adopted during the period.

Operation of Exchange Controls by the Central Bank.

Major policy actions of the Central Bank were decided by a seven-member Monetary Board. The Secretary of Finance was the presiding officer, while the other ex-officio members were the governor of the Central Bank, the president of the government-owned Philippine National Bank, and the chairman of the Development Bank of the Philippines. In addition, three members were selected for six-year terms from the general public.[36]

Circular 44, issued on June 12, 1953, set forth the guiding principles to be followed by the Central Bank in the licensing of foreign exchange for the payment of imports. For each six-month period the Central Bank specified not only the total amount of foreign exchange available to each commercial bank, but also the sums available by commodity category and by importers. The year 1952 was established as the base for allocating foreign exchange among importers, but a contingency reserve was also set up to meet the expansion needs of existing producers, the requirements of new producers for machinery and raw materials, the adjustments of quotas for existing importers, and the foreign-exchange requests of new importers. Only Filipino merchants could qualify as new importers. The commodity breakdown, covering 1,865 items, consisted of:

1. Highly essential commodities (30 items), composed chiefly of medical and pharmaceutical products and dairy products.
2. Essential producer goods (560 items), including particularly most machinery, some transport equipment and professional and scientific instruments, most chemical elements and compounds, fertilizers, minerals and base metals, fuels and lubricants, and selected yarns and fabrics.
3. Nonessential producer goods (162 items), comprising hides and

TABLE 2-4

Major Trade, Payments, and Related Economic Policies, 1953–59

June 1953	Expiration of 1951 Import Control Act and placing of entire import-control mechanism under control of Central Bank
	Enactment of new tax exemption law for "new and necessary" industries, covering import taxes as well as internal taxes
Oct. 1953	Repeal of 80 per cent cash-deposit requirement for specified luxury and nonessential items
Jan. 1954	Reduction of rediscount rate from 2 per cent to 1½ per cent
Sept. 1955	Revision of United States–Philippines Trade Agreement which included accelerating rate at which Philippine duties would be levied on imports from the United States and eliminating statutory U.S. influence over management of foreign-exchange matters
	Replacement of 17 per cent excise tax on foreign exchange by gradually declining (1.7 percentage points per annum) tax on imports
	Enactment of "no-dollar import law" permitting certain exports to be bartered for imports outside of exchange system
1957	Tightening of monetary policies by means of two-step (March and September) rise in rediscount rate to 4½ per cent, establishment of ceilings on various categories of loans, and reintroduction in September and December of differential cash-deposit requirements on letters of credit for importation of various types of goods
June 1957	Introduction of new tariff schedule providing for low rates on essential consumer and producer goods and high rates on items classified as nonessential
Feb. 1958	Easing of cash-deposit requirements on letters of credit
Feb. 1959	Further tightening of monetary controls by increasing rediscount rate to 6½ per cent (but establishing lower preferential rates for crop loans and export bills) and raising reserve requirement against demand deposits
July 1959	Imposition of 25 per cent margin fee levied by Central Bank on sales of foreign exchange

skins, essential oils and perfume materials, and selected animal and vegetable oils, chemicals and yarns, fabrics and other materials.

4. Essential consumer goods (125 items), including certain medical preparations, some foods, and selected items of machinery and transport, heating and lighting equipment.

5. Nonessential consumer goods (460 items), including most fruits and vegetables, most beverages and tobacco products, toilet preparations, most leather goods, and many other consumer manufactures.

6. Unclassified goods (528 items), embracing numerous raw materials and a wide variety of manufactures (e.g., clothing, furniture, wood and cork manufactures) deemed to be produced locally in sufficient quantity and of acceptable quality to meet home demand and offered at competitive prices. The importation of items placed in this category was virtually banned, since specific authorization of the Central Bank was required to bring them into the country.

This essentiality classification remained until 1957 when in accordance with a resolution of the National Economic Council two new groups, semiessential producer goods and semiessential consumer goods, were added, and the highly essential class was replaced by a list of decontrolled items. At this time, the three consumer classes were defined as follows: (1) essential consumer goods—basic necessities of food, clothing, shelter, health, and education for low-income families defined as not earning more than $60 per month; (2) semiessential consumer goods—consisting of nonbasic goods for families with earnings of $60–$150 per month; and (3) nonessential consumer goods—luxury items for families earning over $150 per month. On the producer side the specification of the items to be included was: (1) essential producer goods—requirements of industries producing essential consumer goods, export goods, essential and semiessential producer goods and services including raw materials, and essential utility services; (2) semiessential producer goods—requirements of industries producing semiessential consumer goods, certain exports, and semiessential and nonessential producer goods; and (3) nonessential producer goods—requirements of industries producing nonessential consumer goods. In the allocation of foreign exchange an "adequate" supply was to be made available for imports of essential consumer and producer goods; a "limited" supply for semiessential producer goods; a "more limited" supply for semiessential consumer and nonessential producer goods, which was to be made available only after the requests for semiessential producer items were satisfied; and a "very limited" supply for nonessential consumer items. The 1957 resolution also reaffirmed a policy already in effect in 1954,[37] namely, that notwithstanding these priorities, "foreign exchange shall be made available only to the extent that the commodity proposed to be imported or any suitable substitute is not produced locally."

The main effect of placing all import control operations within the Central Bank was to improve the administrative efficiency of these activities rather than bring about any fundamental change in policy direction. In particular, import-substituting activities were vigorously and consistently pursued throughout the rest of the 1950s. As is noted in the 1954 *Annual Report* of the Central Bank, this was done by the "virtual decontrol of raw materials and machinery and the curtailment of foreign exchange allocations for commodities produced locally in sufficient quantities." At the same time controls on highly essential foods and medicines were eased, with the result that by 1957 all of these items were decontrolled and thus could be imported in unlimited quantities.[38]

TABLE 2-5

**Number of Items Shifted from One Import Classification
to Another Between 1953 and 1958**

To	From							
	DC	HE	EP	EC	NEP	NEC	UI	Total
DC		11		13		1		25
HE								
EP		1		16	5	3		25
EC		1						1
SEP			107	33	51	5	5	201
SEC				5	1	9		15
NEP			12	1		40	4	57
NEC			4	12			2	18
UI			9	14	6	38		67
Total		13	132	94	63	96	11	409

DC = decontrolled items.
HE = highly essential items.
EP = essential producer goods.
EC = essential consumer goods.
SEP = semiessential producer goods.

SEC = semiessential consumer goods.
NEP = nonessential producer goods.
NEC = nonessential consumer goods.
UI   = unclassified items.

NOTE: Categories are arranged from left to right and from top to bottom in roughly descending order of priority for allocation of foreign exchange for imports.
SOURCE: Central Bank of the Philippines.

These points are brought out in Table 2-5, in which are shown the changes made in the classification of goods between 1953 and December 1958. In the consumer goods classes, for example, 52 of the 190 shifts moved items into the unclassified list and thus resulted in the virtual banning of these imports. Articles so affected included writing ink, typewriter ribbons, sausages, roasted coffee, smoking tobacco, waxes and polishes, knitted fabrics, blankets, carpets, incandescent lamps, automobiles, cotton gloves, and lead pencils. At the same time such basic items as canned milk, canned fish, wheat flour, corned beef, and antibiotics (in bulk) were completely decontrolled. It also appears from the table that the exchange authorities must have sought to encourage the domestic production of many simply processed intermediate producer goods, since a large number of items were transferred to the semiessential producer category. The growing emphasis on reducing imports of both consumption goods and nonessential producer goods in favor of essential producer goods is further brought out in Table 2-6, which contains the percentage distribution of import values on the basis of the 1957 exchange-control classification system. Between 1954 and 1959 imports of essential producer goods rose from 40 to 61 per cent of all imports.

As the above descriptions of the 1953 and 1957 exchange-control classes indicate, the criteria for allocating foreign exchange among commodity categories remained essentially unchanged throughout the 1950s. Consumption commodities regarded as necessary to maintain adequate nutritional and health levels for the population were imported very freely, whereas commodities considered to be nonessential luxury items were admitted very sparingly. The key change in the 1957 classification system was that it determined the difficult question of just how one should grade consumption goods by degree of essentiality on the basis of observed consumption patterns by level of income. In the 1957 system also, the goal was to direct a larger share of producer goods imports into the production of the more essential consumer and producer goods categories and of exports. However, in the 1953 and 1957 classifications, the practice was continued of virtually banning imports of an item that exchange-control authorities thought could be produced competitively within the country. The fundamental point to be made about the exchange-control system, however, is that its continued effect was to encourage the domestic production of the very items regarded as nonessential by the authorities.

Another feature of the operation of exchange controls during this period was the increasing Filipinization of the import trade. Between 1948 and 1958, the value of imports traded by Filipinos rose from 23 per cent to 54 per cent. The import share of American importers only declined from 28 per cent to 24 per cent between these years, but the share attributable to Chinese traders fell from 39 per cent to 14 per cent.[39] However, part of the trade classified as being undertaken by Filipino importers was in fact carried out by regular, non-Filipino importers. New Filipino importers sold their import licenses to these regular importers for substantial gains.[40]

TABLE 2-6

Imports Classified by Official Category, 1954–63
(percentage of total imports)

Year	Essential Producer	Semiessential Producer	Nonessential Producer	Essential Consumer	Semiessential Consumer	Nonessential Consumer	Unclassified	Decontrolled
1954	40.2	16.5	7.9	2.1	1.1	6.8	12.6	12.7
1955	46.5	11.6	8.4	3.9	0.7	5.3	9.5	14.0
1956	54.8	12.1	6.8	2.5	0.5	3.2	5.6	14.4
1957	52.0	12.2	6.9	3.4	0.7	3.5	8.0	13.2
1958	50.4	12.4	4.9	4.9	0.5	0.8	7.1	18.9
1959	61.3	11.9	3.7	1.1	0.6	1.1	7.1	13.1
1960	59.4	10.2	4.8	2.0	0.4	1.1	6.7	15.3
1961	60.2	9.4	6.2	1.6	0.5	1.6	6.8	13.7
1962	64.0	11.9	6.9	1.3	0.5	1.8	5.4	8.2
1963	59.7	11.3	7.5	1.4	0.6	2.7	8.3	8.5

SOURCE: Central Bank of the Philippines, *Statistical Bulletin*, March 1964, as cited by Gerardo P. Sicat, "Industrial Policy and the Development of Manufacturing in the Philippines" (University of the Philippines, School of Economics, Institute of Economic Development and Research, Discussion Paper 65-1, January 6, 1965).

Monetary and Fiscal Policies.

The same year (1953) in which the Central Bank assumed full authority for quantitatively controlling imports was also an election year. The Central Bank responded to the consequent pressures for easy exchange-control and credit policies by repealing the 80 per cent cash-deposit requirement for imports of specified luxury and nonessential items and by reducing the required ratio of net foreign-exchange holdings, cash in bank vaults, excess reserves, etc., to letters of credit from 70 to 50 per cent. Furthermore, government spending was significantly increased, and the internal government debt rose 45 per cent.

These expansionary policies were continued after the election of President Ramon Magsaysay, who immediately recommended that a truly integrated development program be planned and put into effect by the National Economic Council.[41] In order to finance the governmental portion of the resulting plan, the Congress authorized the President to borrow up to P1 billion. As part of the general expansionary program, the rediscount rate was lowered in January 1954 from 2 per cent to 1½ per cent per year. Since the capacity of the private sector to absorb government bonds was slight, most of the newly issued government debt ended up in the hands of the Central Bank. For example, in 1954–55 the expenditures of the government for development purposes totaled P331 million, of which P250 million was borrowed from the banking system. In 1955–56 and 1956–57 development expenditures[42] were P467 million and P488 million, with borrowings of P152 million and P129 million, respectively.[43] The money supply increased at an average annual rate of 9.2 per cent from 1954 to 1957. However, real GNP rose at an average annual rate of 6.7 per cent between these years, and the wholesale price index increased at an average yearly rate of only 1.6 per cent.

Central Bank authorities were, however, concerned about the potential inflationary effect of the monetary and expenditure expansion and did succeed in obtaining a credit tightening in 1957. The rediscount rate was raised from 1½ to 2 per cent in March and to 4½ per cent in September. The rate of interest paid on savings deposits was also raised from 2 per cent to 3 per cent in September. Furthermore, in April 1957 the Central Bank adopted a system of priorities on credits to commercial banks and imposed ceilings on the various categories established.[44] But it was not until after the presidential election, in November, that the pressures on the trade balance could be eased by significantly tightening import controls. The deficit on the trade account reached $182 million, the highest since 1949.

The main restraining measure adopted was the reintroduction of margin requirements on letters of credit, in September of 1957. A cash deposit of 100 per cent was required for imports of goods classified as nonessential. In December, imports of decontrolled items, essential consumer and producer goods, and semiessential producer goods were also made subject to the 100 per cent margin requirement, and imports of semiessential consumer and non-essential producer goods, to a 200 per cent margin requirement. Also at that time the opening of letters of credit for nonessential consumer goods, including those purchased through barter, was prohibited.[45]

As the balance of payments quickly improved, most of these measures were relaxed. In February 1958, margin requirements were lifted for imports of decontrolled items and for imports by essential and semiessential producers. In October the margin requirement was reduced from 200 per cent to 100 per cent for semiessential consumer goods and nonessential producer goods. In early 1959, imports of nonessential consumer goods were permitted, first only on a barter basis and then on a normal payment basis. However, a 100 per cent margin requirement was established for such imports.

At the same time that the Central Bank moved to ease its very stringent import controls, it also took various actions to curtail excess demand and reduce windfalls. The rediscount rate was raised in February 1959 from 4½ per cent to 6½ per cent with preferential rates of 4½ per cent given to agricultural crop loans and 5 per cent on export bills. In addition, the reserve requirement against demand deposits was raised in stages from 18 per cent to 21 per cent. Most important, however, was the imposition in July 1959, under R.A. 2609, of a 25 per cent "margin fee" levied by the Central Bank on sales of foreign exchange. The fee was not a tax in that it accrued to the Central Bank rather than the government. The level of this fee was reduced to 20 per cent in November 1960, 15 per cent in March 1961, and finally abolished in January 1962, though, as we shall see in the next chapter, its place was taken by other measures of depreciation.

The 25 per cent levy on foreign exchange was designed not merely to curtail the excess demand problem of the period but also to serve as a significant but uniform cushioning measure for the exchange decontrol that the government had finally decided to undertake.[46] Toward this end, by the act establishing the margin fee, the Central Bank was permitted to set the rate as high as 40 per cent, with the stipulation that application of the rate must be uniform. There were a number of exemptions from the fee, e.g., drugs and medicines, medical and hospital supplies, canned milk, and fertilizers, but significantly they did not include "new and necessary" industries. This move away from preferential treatment for these industries as well as other long-favored groups was further extended by two other laws, approved in June 1959 (R.A. 2351 and R.A. 2352), that eliminated the exemptions of "new and necessary" industries from the special import tax in force since 1955 as well as from the income tax.

As the preceding description indicates, during the 1950s (and also the

1960s) the government did not hesitate to employ deficit spending and easy credit policies either to improve the re-election probabilities of the party in power or to implement a particular development program. Consequently, the Central Bank alternately pursued liberal and restrictive monetary policies. At the outset of a new administration, for example, it would be required to provide credit on a liberal basis in order to stimulate economic growth. However, when this overly liberal monetary policy resulted in strong inflationary pressures as well as serious balance-of-payments problems, the Central Bank would attempt to solve these problems by quickly applying such restrictive monetary policies as higher rediscount rates and cash-deposit requirements for letters of credit.

Increases in Tariff Levels.

As the expiration date (1954) for the period of mutual free trade under the U.S.-Philippine Trade Agreement of 1946 approached, the Philippine government requested a re-examination and adjustment of various provisions of the agreement. The agreement was widely criticized in the Philippines on the grounds that it prevented the Philippines from exercising control over its own exchange rate, resulted in a sizable loss of potential tariff revenue, and granted the country a considerably smaller margin of preference in U.S. markets than initially because of subsequent U.S. tariff cuts. The result of the ensuing negotiations—and after the free trade period had been extended to the end of 1955—was the Revised Trade Agreement, better known as the Laurel-Langley Agreement. This new agreement accelerated the rate at which imports from the United States would be subject to the full amount of Philippine tariffs, while slowing down the initial rise in the application of U.S. tariffs to imports from the Philippines. Specifically, the percentage of each country's tariff rates applicable to imports from the other was set as follows (in place of the annual increases of five percentage points under the 1946 agreement):

Period	Philippine Imports from the United States	U.S. Imports from the Philippines
1956–58	25%	5%
1959–61	50	10
1962–64	75	20
1965–67		40
1968–70	90	60
1971–73		80
After 1973	100	100

Besides these tariff changes, the absolute quota imposed by the United

States on rice was dropped, and those on cigars and scrap tobacco, coconut oil, and pearl buttons were turned into tariff quotas. The sugar and cordage quotas were retained, but the United States agreed that additional sugar quotas, when these became necessary, would be extended to the Philippines.[47] In return for these various concessions, the Philippines agreed to replace the 17 per cent excise tax on foreign-exchange sales with a 17 per cent tax on imports that was reduced 10 per cent i.e., 1.7 percentage points, each year from 1957 on. This change represented an important concession to American investors as well as shipping and insurance companies.

In addition to accelerating the rate at which the full height of Philippine tariffs would be attained against U.S. imports, the government also took steps to raise the level of these duties. The tariff schedule that went into effect after the war was essentially that which had prevailed since 1909. This schedule had been constructed mainly with revenue considerations in mind and was aimed at an ad valorem tariff level of about 23 per cent on dutiable imports from countries other than the United States. Since it was felt that this tariff schedule did not encourage the kind of industrialization sought by the government, a Tariff Commission was created, in 1953 (R.A. 911), and charged with making a thorough study of the duty structure. The Laurel-Langley Agreement went into effect before the Philippine Congress could agree on a new set of tariffs; so the President raised duties by executive order as of January 1, 1956.[48] However, a new tariff code finally was agreed upon and went into effect in June 1957. Under the new law not only were duty rates changed, but the President was given the authority to raise tariffs up to 400 per cent of their new levels or lower them by 50 per cent after an investigation by the Tariff Commission.

Under the 1957 act, duties were lowered on essential consumer goods (e.g., canned milk) and on essential raw materials and producer goods (e.g., tractor fuels and machinery) that were not likely to be produced in adequate supply domestically in the foreseeable future. On the other hand, they were raised on nonessentials and goods for which import-substitution possibilities were regarded as favorable (e.g., textile products and paper and paperboard manufactures). Valdepeñas calculated the following 1957 nominal tariff averages for a sample of 111 commodities classified by the essentiality categories of the Central Bank: highly essential goods, 15 per cent; essential consumer goods, 18 per cent; nonessential consumer goods, 51 per cent; essential producer goods, 25 per cent; nonessential producer goods, 30 per cent.[49] The distribution of dutiable items by tariff levels is shown in Table 2-7 for the 1949 and 1957 tariff schedules as well as for the rates prevailing in 1970. As this table shows, a number of duties were lowered in 1957, but so, too, were a number raised. On balance the simple average of duties rose from 23 per cent in 1949 to 36 per cent in 1957. A consideration of tariff changes by major

TABLE 2-7

Distribution of Ad Valorem Duties, 1949, 1957, 1970

Percentage Range of Ad Valorem Rates	Percentage of Dutiable Items[a]		
	1949	1957	1970
0–5.0	1.0	1.8	1.8
5.1–10.0	12.5	29.9	26.8
10.1–15.0	18.1	9.8	9.3
15.1–20.0	13.8	8.2	8.0
20.1–25.0	21.0	8.7	7.6
25.1–30.0	11.2	3.1	4.0
30.1–40.0	13.5	7.1	7.3
40.1–50.0	5.6	6.8	7.5
50.1–60.0	2.0	4.3	5.7
60.1–90.0	1.0	8.0	9.5
90.1–100.0	0.3	9.0	8.8
100.1–250.0	0	3.4	3.6
	100.0	100.0	100.0
Mean rate	22.8	36.2	37.7

SOURCE: Philippine Tariff Commission.

a. In 1949, the ad valorem schedule included only about 300 items; by 1957 and 1970, the number had risen to about 1,200.

commodity categories from 1949 to 1957 brings out that for such simple manufactures as textiles and prepared foodstuffs tariffs were sharply increased, whereas for raw materials groups, such as chemicals, or capital goods categories, such as mechanical and electrical equipment, they were reduced on many items. The following description of the tariff structure, taken from a document prepared by the Tariff Commission, aptly describes not only the pattern of tariff protection, but also the protection pattern afforded by the exchange-control system of the 1950s.

The height of duties, however, for different classes of products varies according to several factors, namely, essentiality of the articles, availability of the articles locally and comparability quality-wise of domestically produced articles with the imported. Essential articles may be either consumer or producer goods. Non-essentials include luxuries and articles normally consumed by the high-income consumers. On the basis of these factors, the structure of the Philippine tariff may be broadly described as follows:

1. Low rates are provided for essential consumer goods and essential producer goods which are not produced locally in sufficient quantity and of the desired quality.
    a) The essential consumer goods in this category consist of products which are consumed by the general mass of the people and necessary for their health and well-being.
    b) Essential producer goods include raw materials and intermediate goods used in the manufacture of locally made articles. Machineries, equipment and supplies used in domestic production also belong to the category of essential producer goods.
2. On the other hand, high rates of duty are imposed on luxuries and non-essential articles.
3. Protective duties are levied on articles produced locally in substantial quantity and acceptable quality. The level of the duty is considered according to the nature of the protected article, the production capacity of the local industry to meet the domestic demand, cost equalization, labor, raw materials, capitalization and other economic factors.[50]

When the 1957 Tariff Act was put into effect its main impact was to capture for the government a greater share of the windfall gains associated with the quantitative limitation of many imports through exchange controls. However, as is brought out in Chapter 5, when exchange controls were dismantled, in the early 1960s, and tariffs became effective constraints on import prices, the pattern of low duties on basic consumer goods, raw materials, and capital goods and high rates on luxuries and other nonessential goods continued to provide the same general structure of protection as existed under exchange controls.

Tax and Financial Assistance to Industry.

The policy of import substitution was further strengthened in the early 1950s by the enactment in 1953 of a new tax exemption law (R.A. 901) for "new and necessary" industries. The new law covered not only internal taxes but, unlike the 1946 law, it also covered external taxes (i.e., import duties, the sales tax, and the 17 per cent excise tax on foreign exchange). The extent of the tax exemption was 100 per cent through 1958, 90 per cent in 1959, 75 per cent in 1960, 50 per cent in 1961, and 10 per cent in 1962, after which the privilege expired. Not only did firms covered by the old act automatically receive the new benefits, but also firms whose exemption period had expired could apply anew for the privileges. The qualifications for "new" and "necessary" industries were similar to those of the previous law. A "new" industry was one not in existence on a commercial basis before January 1, 1945, and a "necessary" industry was one that would: (1) "contribute to the attainment of a stable and balanced national economy," [51] (2) "operate in comformity with up-to-date practices" and give promise of "a reasonable degree of permanency," and (3) use imported raw materials that "do not exceed 60 percent of manufacturing cost plus reasonable selling and administrative expenses." Under the previous law a 50 per cent import-component ceiling had been imposed for raw materials.[52] During the six years (1953–58) when the exemption rate was 100 per cent, the tax exemption law of 1953 resulted in tax savings equivalent to 12.1 per cent of the annual sales of the firms involved.[53] This figure gradually decreased thereafter, e.g., to 9.1 per cent in 1960, until firms were liable to the full tax rate in 1963.

As already noted, the early response to the 1946 tax exemption law was disappointing; and it was not until tight import controls began, in 1950, that any significant number of entrepreneurs took advantage of the law. In 1950, 13 firms were granted tax exemptions, and by 1952, the number had risen to 48. After the revisions in 1953, the number rose to 321 in 1955 and 900 in 1958. The output of these 900 firms was P650 million, or 21 per cent of the gross output of all manufacturing firms in 1958.[54] The commodity distribution of the tax-exempt firms as of 1957 is shown in Table 2-8. It can be seen that the assistance provided under the tax-exemption program up to that date especially favored producers of nonessential consumer goods.

TABLE 2-8

Tax-exempt Industries in the Philippines Classified by
the Essentiality of Their Products, 1957

Product Category	Number of Enterprises	Per Cent
Nonessential producers	49	6.3
Semiessential producers	118	16.1
Essential producers	228	29.5
Nonessential consumers	268	34.7
Semiessential consumers	29	3.1
Essential consumers	78	10.1
Decontrolled	2	0.2
Total	772	100.0

SOURCE: Jack Heller and Kenneth M. Kauffman, *Tax Incentives for Industry in Less Developed Countries* (Cambridge: Harvard Law School, 1963), Table VI, p. 121, as reported in G. P. Sicat, "Industrial Policy and the Development of Manufacturing in the Philippines" (University of the Philippines, School of Economics, Institute of Economic Development and Research, Discussion Paper 65-1, January 5, 1965), p. 32.

Still another impetus to economic development during this period stemmed from the easy long-term credit policies of various Philippine and international financing organizations. The Rehabilitation Finance Corporation (RFC),[55] for example, made loans totaling $788 million (P1,576 million) between 1947 and 1957, of which 55 per cent went to agriculture, 19 per cent to industry, 23 per cent for real estate construction and repair, 2 per cent for self-liquidating government projects, and 1 per cent for miscellaneous purposes.[56] The lending rate of the RFC was about 2 per cent below that prevailing in private markets.

Economic assistance from the United States and Japan also furthered the development and import-substitution goals of the Philippines. During the 1946–52 period American aid amounted to $777 million—$670 million in grants and $107 million in loans.[57] This early aid was used mainly for rebuilding and to meet urgent needs for consumption goods. Between 1953 and 1965 the aid figure came to $333 million, of which $260 million represented grants and $73 million, loans.[58] In allocating aid in this period, greater emphasis was placed on the industrialization goals of the country.[59] One-quarter of the aid went for industrial purposes. Other uses of this assistance were: food relief, 16 per cent; communications, 10 per cent; health and education, 12 per cent; community development, public administration, and miscellaneous purposes, 10 per cent. The government of Japan agreed in 1956 to make reparations to the Philippines equivalent to $550 million in capital goods, services, and cash over a twenty-year period. By April 1965 the sum received was $144 million. The main recipients were the shipping industry, the railroads, the Public Works Department, and the cement, textile, and paper and pulp industries.[60]

Encouraging Exports.

Few specific measures were taken in the 1950s to stimulate exports, and it was the pressure of traditional exporters that played a large role in finally bringing about the devaluations of the early 1960s. As is shown in Chapter 5, during the 1950s exporters suffered a significant decline in domestic purchasing power. The main policy taken to offset in part the penalty on exporters of an overvalued exchange rate was the enactment of the so-called No-Dollar Import Law of 1955 (R.A. 1410). Under this law, certain exports could be bartered for imports outside the exchange control system. The first set of rules limited barter transactions to "minor" exports, to any excess over the U.S. quotas for goods covered by the trade agreement between the two countries, and to any excess over the preceding five-year export average for all other goods. Presumably, the effective exchange rate for these barter transactions was at about the black-market exchange rate of P3 per dollar. Permitted imports were mainly restricted to producer goods and essential raw materials. In 1957 barter exports amounted to 10 per cent of total exports. After considerable oscillation in the rules covering allowable transactions and because of the strong opposition both of protected importers and the Central Bank, the law was repealed in 1959. However, a new law (R.A. 2261), An Act to Promote Economic Development by Giving Incentives to Marginal and Submarginal Industries, was passed in its place and specified a list of items as eligible for barter trade (subject to the conditions that they could not be sold profitably for dollars and were in adequate supply to meet local requirements).[61] In addition, the National Economic Council was directed to recommend annually to the Congress any additional industries that should be covered by the act.

Gold producers, who had accounted for about one-quarter of Philippine exports in the prewar period, were another group accorded preferential treatment under the exchange-control system. The details of the country's gold policy varied during the period, but its main features were a direct subsidy and permission to sell a portion of production in the higher-priced free market for gold rather than to the Central Bank. As Golay points out, in the years 1949–57, over 80 per cent of the country's production was sold on the free market.[62] Its average price was about $55 per ounce of gold rather than the official price of $35 an ounce.

Undervaluation of exports was a persistent problem throughout the period of tight exchange control as Philippine citizens used exports as a means of attempting to transfer funds abroad in expectation of a devaluation, to circumvent the limitation on funds available for foreign travel, or to diversify their foreign investment portfolios. Consequently, the export licensing system established as part of the exchange-control system was gradually tightened and made more elaborate. Exporters were eventually required to submit detailed evidence as to the quantity and kind or grade of the commodity exported, which was then authenticated at the port of discharge. Officials in the Export Department also undertook a thorough analysis of the proposed export prices before granting an export license. Despite these efforts, it was estimated by the Central Bank itself that at least 10 per cent of the dollar receipts from exports remained abroad rather than being turned over to the Central Bank.

NOTES

1. Paul V. McNutt, *United States High Commissioner to [the] Philippine Islands— —Final Report*, U.S. Congress, *House Document*, vol. IX (389), 80th Cong., 1st sess., 1947, pp. 20–21.
2. Central Bank of the Philippines, *Second Annual Report*, 1950, p. 15.

3. In 1945 the country's exports amounted to less than $1 million and its imports to $29 million. See R. Garcia, "Exchange Rate Policy in the Philippines," *Central Bank News Letter*, July 26, 1966.

4. See Philippine Economic Survey Mission *Revised Philippine Economic Development Program* (1950; dittoed).

5. The agreement also stipulated that Philippine exports of sugar, cordage, rice, cigars, scrap tobacco, coconut oil, and buttons of pearl shell were to be subject to absolute quotas in the U.S. market throughout the entire period of the agreement.

6. Agreement between the United States of America and the Republic of the Philippines, Article V, U.S. Department of State, *Treaties and Other International Acts*, Series 1588 (not dated).

7. Frank H. Golay, *The Philippines: Public Policy and National Economic Development* (Ithaca: Cornell University Press, 1961), p. 64. This U.S. legislation provided the Philippines with $620 million for war damages.

8. Still another attempt to increase the supplies of essential goods available for domestic purchasers was the imposition of export controls through Executive Order 192 in December 1948. This restricted the exportation of vital foodstuffs, important industrial goods, and a few construction materials. However, the Supreme Court of the Philippines declared the order null and void because it violated the Philippine Trade Act of 1946.

9. Examples of items included on this list were beer, wines, whiskey, automobiles, perfumes and other toilet preparations, toys, wool, silk and synthetic woven fabrics and ready-made wearing apparel, radios, boots and shoes, cigarettes, and fresh fruit.

10. Vicente B. Valdepeñas, Jr., *The Protection and Development of Philippine Manufacturing* (Manila: Ateneo University Press, 1970), Table 4.2, p. 56.

11. This relationship is analyzed in more detail in Chapter 6.

12. Miguel Cuaderno, Sr., *Problems of Economic Development (The Philippines— A Case Study)* (Manila: privately published, 1961), p. 20.

13. Valdepeñas, *Philippine Manufacturing*, p. 57.

14. An increase in the magnitude of the errors and omission item in the balance of payments from a debit level of $48 million in 1948 to $93 million in 1949 supports this view.

15. The reserve requirement for demand deposits remained unchanged at 18 per cent from 1949 to 1959. Little use has been made of open-market operations in the Philippines because of the absence of a significant bond market.

16. Valdepeñas, *Philippine Manufacturing*, p. 29.

17. Loc. cit.

18. Such consumption commodities as corned beef, fresh and frozen meat, spices, medicines, rubber boots and shoes, and jute bags were on this short list.

19. Butter, cheese, raw coffee, tea, hams, inexpensive cotton, silk and rayon textiles, cotton and rayon yarns, fresh oranges, apples, grapes and lemons, electrical batteries, nails, inexpensive radios, refrigerators, paints, and commercial explosives illustrate the type of commodities on this list.

20. Examples of such goods were bakery products, breakfast foods, fresh and canned fish, canned and dried fruits, canned and dried meat, tobacco products, electric stoves, musical instruments, lamps, writing paper, phonograph records, table and kitchen utensils, and inexpensive watches.

21. Leather manufactures, air-conditioning equipment, automobiles, small cameras, furs, whiskey and wines, phonographs, perfumes, sporting goods, toys, fresh and canned vegetables, and wood manufactures were among the items included in this list.

22. Golay, *The Philippines,* p. 28.

23. For example, the bank permitted students studying abroad to use a maximum of $2,400 per year for all living expenses exclusive of tuition and other expenses payable to the educational institution. Funds for the latter purpose were made available, but it was required that they be paid directly to the institution. For persons other than students situated abroad, a maximum of $200 per month was permitted for the necessary living expenses of each authorized beneficiary or dependent residing in North, Central, or South America, $50 per month for each such person in Asia, and $150 for each one residing in other countries. Payments of life insurance premiums on nonpeso policies were permitted if in force before December 9, 1949, but new or extended policies required the approval of the Central Bank.

24. Valdepeñas, *Philippine Manufacturing,* Table 3.1, p. 30.

25. See Golay, *The Philippines,* pp. 222–226; and Amado Castro, "Central Bank of the Philippines" (1970; mimeo.), p. 4.

26. Central Bank of the Philippines, *Annual Report,* 1951, p. 15.

27. Even the prices of controlled items rose above their established ceilings. The Central Bank found, for example, that in March of 1951, for a selected sample of 60 commodities, actual retail prices exceeded their ceiling levels by an average of 10.3 per cent.

28. Central Bank of the Philippines, *Annual Report,* 1951, p. 9.

29. Economic Survey Mission to the Philippines, *Report to the President of the United States* (Washington, D.C., October 5, 1950).

30. Central Bank of the Philippines, *Annual Report,* 1951, pp. 14–15.

31. Specifically, tax refunds were made on such foodstuffs as rice, flour, canned meat and fish, cattle and beef, and on textbooks and a long list of medicines and medical supplies.

32. As is further explained in the section on tariff changes, this 17 per cent excise tax on foreign exchange was replaced in 1957 by a 17 per cent special import tax on commodities. Furthermore, beginning in 1957, this tax decreased by 1.7 percentage points each year until it was finally eliminated in 1966.

33. Virginia Yapinchay, "General Theories and Mechanics of Trade Restrictions with Emphasis on Philippine Experience," *Central Bank News Digest,* June 14, 1955; Valdepeñas, *Philippine Manufacturing,* p. 60.

34. For an elaboration of these charges, see Caridad Carreon Semana, "Some Political Aspects of Philippine Economic Development" (Ph.D. diss., Harvard University, June 1965). Apparently payments to government officials amounted in some cases to as much as 50 per cent of the value of foreign exchange licenses. See A. V. H. Hartendorp, *History of Industry and Trade of the Philippines; the Magsaysay Administration* (Manila: Philippine Education Press, 1961), pp. 300–301.

35. Imports under "no-dollar remittance" referred to commodities for which no foreign-exchange allocation was made by the Central Bank.

36. In November 1972 the chairman of the Central Bank was made chairman of the Monetary Board. In addition, the president of the Philippine National Bank and the chairman of the Development Bank were replaced by the director-general of the National Economic Development Authority and the chairman of the Board of Investments.

37. Speech by A. Jison, reported in *Central Bank News Digest,* November 16, 1954.

38. Speech by I. M. Cuaderno, reported in *Central Bank News Digest,* March 26, 1957.

39. Golay, *The Philippines,* p. 318.

40. A. V. H. Hartendorp, *History of Industry and Trade of the Philippines* (Manila: American Chamber of Commerce of the Philippines, 1958), p. 678.

41. The function of the National Economic Council was to coordinate government economic policies.

42. Development expenditures by the government were concentrated on the construction of schools, hospitals, hydroelectric projects, communication facilities, and irrigation systems.

43. Cuaderno, *Problems of Economic Development,* p. 121.

44. In order of priority the categories were: Priority I, industrial loans; Priority II, public utility loans; Priority III, real estate loans; and Priority IV, consumption loans.

45. Imports of essential producer raw materials for industrial plants approved by the Central Bank and National Economic Council plus essential industries established before December 9, 1949, required only a 50 per cent margin requirement, and capital goods imports under deferred payment arrangements only a 25 per cent requirement. Another important feature of this restraining measure was the clause stating that imports "by the Philippine Government, its subdivisions, instrumentalities, government owned and controlled corporations and all other government agencies and importations under U.S. Public Law 480 and all ICA imports shall be given the same treatment as ordinary imports."

46. President Garcia stated in a speech on July 2, 1959, that over a three- or four-year period there would be a substantial relaxation of controls. Reported in *Central Bank News Digest,* July 14, 1959, pp. 4–5.

47. Valdepeñas, *Philippine Manufacturing,* p. 78.

48. His authority for doing so was based upon a 1954 law permitting him to raise tariffs by 100 per cent or reduce them by 60 per cent.

49. Valdepeñas, *Philippine Manufacturing,* p. 81.

50. Philippine Tariff Commission, "General View of the Present Philippine Tariff Structure" (July 31, 1970; mimeo.).

51. Industries listed in the appendix attached to the act as being conducive to its objective of attaining "a stable and balanced" economy were iron and steel products, processed local fuels, chemicals, copper and copper alloy products, refractors, processed foods, textile and fiber manufactures from local raw materials, fertilizers, agricultural equipment, refrigeration and air-conditioning equipment, raw plastic materials, porcelain products, paper and paper products, medical and pharmaceutical products, rubber manufacturers, electric motors, office and school equipment and supplies, household and kitchen utensils, and industrial abrasives.

52. John H. Power and Gerardo P. Sicat, *The Philippines: Industrialization and Trade Policies* (London: Oxford University Press, 1971), p. 80.

53. Philippine Chamber of Industries, *Official Proceedings,* Fifth National Convention of Manufacturers and Producers, Volume VIII, 1958.

54. Calculated from Philippine Chamber of Industries, *Official Proceedings;* and Philippine Bureau of the Census and Statistics, *Preliminary Report on BCS Annual Survey of Manufactures,* 1958, Tables 1 and 2.

55. In 1958, the name of this organization was changed to the Development Bank of the Philippines and its lending resources were increased.

56. Rehabilitation Finance Corporation, *Ten Years of the RFC* (Manila, 1957).

57. U.S. AID Mission to the Philippines, *A Survey of Foreign Economic Assistance Programs in the Philippines,* October 1964, p. 50.

58. Loc. cit.

59. Golay, *The Philippines,* pp. 299–300.

60. U.S. AID Mission, *Survey of Assistance,* p. 37.

61. The following items were specified: ore and concentrates of copper, iron, chrome, manganese, quicksilver, coal, muscovado sugar, embroidery, pearl buttons, low-grade hemp, saw logs, low-grade veneers and lumber, railway ties, industrial salt, cassava and products made thereof, snake and crocodile skulls, and peanuts.

62. Golay, *The Philippines,* p. 160.

Chapter 3

Decontrol and Devaluation, 1960–65

Continuing pressure from export producers, dissatisfaction with the way in which exchange controls were being administered, and a general disillusionment with the system because of its failure to maintain the high growth rates of the early 1950s finally led to a gradual easing of exchange controls and depreciation of the peso. The first section of this chapter contains a description of the various decontrol steps taken from 1960 through 1965; the economic effects of the liberalization effort are analyzed in the second section.

DECONTROL MEASURES

The major steps taken in the first two years of the liberalization period, i.e., Phase III in the Bhagwati-Krueger schema of exchange-control stages, are summarized in Table 3-1.

The Introduction of Multiple Exchange Rates.

Formal decontrol and liberalization began in April 1960 when the Central Bank introduced multiple exchange rates under Circular 105. Two rates were set: an official rate (later called the "preferred" rate), which equaled the existing rate of P2 per dollar, and a "free-market" rate which was initially set at P3.2 per dollar. "Free market" was a misnomer, since this rate was rigidly maintained by the Central Bank, to which all foreign exchange still had to be surrendered. The actual exchange rate that applied to sales of foreign

TABLE 3-1

Major Trade, Payments, and Related Economic Policies, 1960–61

April 1960	Establishment of multiple-rate system in which exchange rate on dollar, including margin fee, ranged between P2.5 for imports of essential goods to P4 for nonessential imports. Exchange rate for exports set at P2.3 per dollar.
Sept. 1960	Modification of "free-market" rate so that the most depreciated rate (i.e., that for nonessential imports) including margin fee was reduced to P3.75 per dollar. Export rate unchanged.
Nov. 1960	Increase in proportion of transactions taking place at "free-market" rate plus reduction of margin fee from 25 per cent to 20 per cent. Exchange rate on dollar including margin fee ranged from P2.4 for imports of highly essential goods and P2.5 for exports to P3.6 for imports of nonessential commodities.
June, Sept., and Nov. 1960	Reduction of rediscount rate in three stages from 6½ per cent to 5 per cent. Reserve requirement also decreased.
March 1961	Further increases in share of transactions taking place at P3 to the dollar. Margin fee reduced to 15 per cent. Thus, rate on dollar, including margin, ranged from P2.75 for exports and P2.87 for imports of highly essential goods to P3.45 for most transactions.
May 1961	Additional easing of credit conditions by decreasing rediscount rate to 3 per cent and further reductions in required reserve ratio.
June 1961	Passage of new tax exemption law permitting many major domestic manufacturing industries to waive import taxes on imports of machinery and equipment.

exchange to the Central Bank depended upon the proportions at which this exchange could be converted at the official and "free-market" rates. The initial proportions for purchases of exchange by the Central Bank are shown in Table 3-2.

Foreign exchange from the Central Bank for imports of items classified as essential consumer goods, semiessential consumer goods, essential producer goods, semiessential producer goods, and decontrolled items could still be purchased at the old rate of P2 to the dollar plus the 25 per cent margin fee on the sale of foreign exchange, i.e., an actual rate of P2.5 to the dollar.[1] All other import transactions took place at the rate of P3.2 per dollar plus the 25 per cent margin requirement.[2] The effective rate on these import transactions, taking account of the 25 per cent margin levy, was thus P4 pesos per dollar.

TABLE 3-2

**Conversion Proportions of Foreign-Exchange Receipts by the Central Bank
at Official and Free-Market Rates, April 1960**

	Percentage to Be Surrendered at		Actual Pesos per Dollar
	Official Rate	Free-Market Rate	
Export receipts	75	25	2.3
Gold proceeds		100	3.2
Tourist receipts		100	3.2
Receipts from other invisibles	75	25	2.3
Receipts from U.S. government	75	25	2.3

SOURCE: Central Bank of the Philippines, *Annual Report*, 1960, p. 267.

It was also stated in Circular 105 that the proportion of transactions at the so-called free-market rate would be gradually increased and the 100 per cent level would be reached not later than 1964. About 25 per cent of all foreign-exchange transactions took place at the "free-market" rate in the first stage of decontrol.

In September 1960, the bank retreated somewhat in the extent to which it allowed the peso to depreciate by fixing the so-called free-market rate at P3 per dollar, exclusive of the margin fee. This reduced the most depreciated import rate from P4.00 to P3.75 per dollar inclusive of the 25 per cent margin. At the same time, however, the actual buying rate by the Central Bank for foreign-exchange receipts from exports, invisibles, and U.S. government transactions was maintained by increasing the proportion of exchange convertible at the free-market rate from 25 per cent to 30 per cent. The margin-deposit requirements introduced in 1957 with Circular 79 and which had been reduced in May were also revoked in September 1960.

The second stage of decontrol by the Central Bank began in November 1960 when changes were made in the proportions at which exchange was allotted at the two rates so as to lessen the gap between buying and selling rates for most classes of transactions. Half of all foreign-exchange receipts from exports, U.S. government expenditures, and invisibles other than those specifically mentioned could be converted into pesos at the preferred (official) rate and half at the free-market rate. The latter rate applied entirely with respect to foreign investments in the country, gold proceeds, foreign tourists' expenditures, and inward remittances of veterans and Filipino citizens as well as the personal expenses of diplomatic personnel. The preferred rate of P2 per dollar still held for imports of decontrolled items, but only 50 per cent of essential producer and essential consumer goods and 40 per cent of semiessential producer goods could be purchased at this rate. About one-half of all transactions took place at the "free-market" rate of P3 to the dollar. An accompanying measure to these changes was the lowering of the margin fee on the sales of foreign exchange by the Central Bank from 25 to 20 per cent.

Various rules were promulgated during the year, permitting foreign exchange to be purchased at the "free-market" rate without prior Central Bank approval. For example, quota-holding producers could purchase exchange at this rate in excess of their quotas, provided the exchange was for imports to be used for the maintenance or expansion of their existing lines of business.

Besides easing exchange controls, the Central Bank pursued a liberal credit policy during 1960 as part of its efforts to stimulate free-market forces and ease the adjustment of producers to the currency depreciation. The rediscount rate was reduced in June from 6½ to 6 per cent, with preferential rates remaining at 4½ and 5 per cent. In September the basic rate dropped to 5¾ per cent and then to 5 per cent in November.[3] The legal reserve requirement against peso demand deposits was also lowered: from 21 to 19 per cent in September, then to 18 per cent in November, and to 17 per cent in December.

As is indicated in Table 5-1, the impact of the various steps taken in 1960 was to increase the effective exchange rate—i.e., the number of pesos actually paid or received per dollar on international transactions of a particular type—by 38 per cent for imports of nonessential consumer goods and by 11 per cent for traditional exports.

Further Depreciation and Additional Adjustment Policies.

The Central Bank began the third phase of its decontrol program, in March 1961, by a currency depreciation for both selling and buying transactions. Seventy-five per cent of export proceeds, exchange from U.S. government transactions, and, subject to certain exceptions, invisibles could be surrendered at the "free-market" rate of P3 per dollar. The conversion ratio at this rate for foreign investment, gold proceeds, etc., remained at 100 per cent. Importers of decontrolled items were permitted to pay the lower preferred rate on 50 per cent (rather than, as before, 100 per cent) of the Central Bank exchange allocations to this category. Twenty-five per cent of the import requirements of dollar-earning industries could also be purchased at the favored P2-per-dollar rate. Except for government expenditures up to June 30, 1961, and forward exchange contracts approved by the Central Bank, sales by the Central Bank for all other purposes took place at the P3-per-dollar rate. This included purchases in excess of licenses granted by the Central Bank. The bank reported that 75 per cent of all foreign-exchange transactions took place at this depreciated rate. Still another liberalizing measure, adopted in March 1961, was a further reduction of the margin fee on foreign-exchange sales from 20 per cent to 15 per cent. At this stage the actual level for the "free-market" rate was thus P3.45 per dollar.

In early 1961, profits and dividends earned on foreign investments approved after January 1, 1960, were permitted to be remitted entirely at the "free-market" rate. The nonremittable part of nonresidents' profits or earlier investments could be used to purchase gold from local producers at a specified subsidy price, i.e., above $35 an ounce, and then exchanged at the Central Bank for foreign exchange at the official rate of $35 per ounce of gold. Foreign technicians and executives employed by firms doing business in the Philippines were allowed to remit abroad up to 50 per cent of their salaries at the "free-market" rate.

A policy of monetary ease continued to be pursued during 1961 despite a reduction in international reserves. The reserve requirement on peso demand deposits was cut from 17 to 16 per cent in January and then to 15 per cent in May. In the same month the rediscount rate for all types of transactions was cut to 3 per cent, and portfolio ceilings on real estate loans were eased. The money supply rose 16 per cent during the year. Because 1961 was a presidential election year, there was also a sharp increase in the government's cash deficit and in borrowing from the Central Bank.

As previously noted, unclassified items (UI) could be imported only when specifically authorized by the Central Bank and in effect were banned. Consequently, one way that the pressures of exchange liberalization were eased for certain industries was by transferring import-competing goods into the UI category. During 1960 and 1961 some twenty-eight commodity lines were transferred to this classification.[4] As of mid-1960, about one-third of all import items (in terms of their classification numbers) were already unclassified.

Local firms engaged in producing refrigerators, air-conditioners, beverage coolers, and other refrigerating units were also helped by a change in the sales tax (or its equivalent for direct users of imports, the compensating tax). The tax on local firms was reduced from 30 per cent to either 15 or 7 per cent, depending upon whether the firm processed a relatively high or low share of raw materials into intermediate inputs. Imported equipment of this type still was taxed at a rate equivalent to 45 per cent.

In addition to being assisted in their adjustment by easy credit, an expansionary fiscal policy, and import-classification changes, most of the key import-substitution industries were helped by the enactment of a new tax-exemption law in 1961—the so-called Basic Industries Act (R.A. 3127). This permitted the special import tax, the compensating sales tax, the margin fee on foreign exchange, and import duties on imports of machinery, spare parts, and equipment to be waived for many major lines of domestic manufacturing as well as several nonmanufacturing activities.[5] However, implementation of the act was delayed by lack of operating funds, and no grant was extended until February 1963. Amendments were made to the act, in both 1964 and 1965, which changed the industry coverage somewhat as well as the schedule of exemptions. As of 1965, a 100 per cent tax exemption was granted through 1967; 75 per cent for 1968 and 1969; and 50 per cent for 1970 and 1971. Thereafter, the full amount of the taxes was to be paid. After 1965 both the margin fee on foreign exchange and the special import tax were lifted, so that the tax exemption applied only to import duties on machinery and spare parts, and to the sales tax. Between 1963 and 1967 exemptions totaling P121 million were granted—a sum that amounted to only 80 per cent of the exemptions granted in the last year (1961) of the old act. The plywood and veneer industry received 25 per cent of the exemptions; the food industry, 24 per cent; and the textile industry, 22 per cent.[6]

During the second year of exchange decontrol (1961) the effective exchange rate for imports of nonessential consumer goods increased less than 1 per cent while the rate for traditional exports increased by 21 per cent. The rates for imports of essential consumer goods and producer goods for "new and necessary" industries rose 40 per cent from 1960 to 1961.

Complete Exchange Decontrol.

With the inauguration of President Diosdado Macapagal, the liberalization timetable of the previous administration was scrapped. Full exchange decontrol was decreed on January 21, 1962, under Circular 133 of the Central Bank. This continued liberalization marks the beginning of Phase IV in the Bhagwati-Krueger schema. The major policy changes that occurred in this period are indicated in Table 3-3. Under the decontrol order licenses were no longer required for any imports, exports, or invisibles. However, the order stipulated that imports (except "no-dollar" imports) must be covered by letters of credit and that a special time deposit must accompany letters of credit. The time-deposit requirement varied with the essentiality classification of imports in the following manner: unclassified items and nonessential consumer goods, 150 per cent; nonessential producer goods and semiessential consumer goods, 100 per cent; semiessential producer goods, 50 per cent; essential consumer goods, essential producer goods, and decontrolled items, 25 per cent. Importers were required to maintain the time deposits in their banks for at least 120 days, and the banks were required to hold reserves on the deposits equivalent to 100 per cent of their value. The margin levy on foreign exchange was suspended.

TABLE 3-3

Major Trade, Payments, and Related Economic Policies, 1962-65

Jan. 1962	Removal of most exchange controls and elimination of margin fee. Peso floated in free market. However, special time-deposit requirements imposed on imports; exporters required to surrender 20 per cent of their foreign-exchange receipts at old rate of P2 per dollar. Import duties on many items raised at same time that exchange controls were lifted.
June 1962	Free-market rate stabilized at P3.90 per dollar. With 20 per cent surrender requirement, rate for exporters became P3.52 per dollar.
Jan. 1962	Both rediscount rate and reserve requirement raised (former to 6 per cent).
1962-64	Some easing of special time-deposit requirement.
Nov. 1965	Elimination of penalty rate for exporters and formal move to unified exchange rate of P3.90 per dollar.

In addition to eliminating virtually all controls, the Central Bank floated the peso in the free market. However, the Central Bank intervened in the market through the Philippine National Bank to prevent excessive short-run fluctuations. All import transactions took place at the free-market rate, but 20 per cent of the receipts from exports and invisibles had to be surrendered to the Central Bank at the official rate of P2 per dollar.[7] Thus, in effect, the bank continued to impose a tax on exporters. The free-market rate rose slowly until May 1962 when it reached a temporary plateau of P3.54 per dollar. However, in June, the rate rose again to around P3.90 per dollar, and the Central Bank supported this rate. The rate remained stable at this level, and in November 1965 the peso was formally devalued from P2 per dollar to P3.90 per dollar.

The unfavorable export rate and the special time deposits were directed primarily at curtailing inflationary forces that could nullify the move toward a more realistic exchange rate. Other anti-inflationary steps were also taken. In January 1962, the rediscount rate for commercial banks was raised from 3 to 6 per cent, and the reserve requirement was increased from 15 to 19 per cent. Later in the year, however, there was some easing of credit controls. In March, the special time deposit was abolished for decontrolled items, essential consumer goods, and essential producer goods. At that time the Central Bank also stipulated that the time-deposit requirement, where applicable, could be made in government securities as well as cash. These changes were followed, in May, by a cut in the time-deposit requirement for unclassified items and nonessential consumer goods from 150 to 100 per cent; for nonessential producer goods and semiessential consumer goods from 100 to 75 per cent; and for semiessential producer goods from 50 to 25 per cent.[8]

The easing of the time-deposit requirement continued into 1963 when imports of machinery, spare parts, and equipment by firms coming under the new tax exemption law of 1961 (R.A. 3127) were exempted from the requirement.[9] A slight concession to exporters was also made in September 1963 by excluding the cost of freight from the export proceeds required to be surrendered to the Central Bank at the official rate. In December 1964 the 20 per cent surrender requirement was further modified to exempt exports with a 1962–63 average annual value of $2 million or less. This represented an attempt to stimulate exports of manufactured goods. Finally, on November 6, 1965, the 20 per cent requirement was completely eliminated, and a unified exchange rate of P3.90 per dollar was officially established.

Besides exempting imports of equipment and raw materials by many new manufacturing industries from the special time-deposit requirement, the government granted special credit arrangements to these industries and increased the tariffs protecting them. In 1962, for example, the 3 per cent preferential rediscount rate of the Central Bank was extended to food processing; textiles; drug-making; veneer, plywood, and prefabricated products; farming and livestock; fisheries; cassava and coconut flour; the marketing and distribution of the foregoing products; and home construction approved by the government. Moreover, at the time that most controls were eliminated, in January 1962, tariffs on nearly 700 articles were raised in order to protect local industries from the greater import competition associated with the decontrol program.[10] Other increases in import duties occurred in later years of the decontrol period. Additional protection against imports from the United States was also provided in 1962 by the scheduled increase from 50 per cent to 75 per cent in the share of Philippine duties applicable to these imports. As provided by the Revised Trade Agreement of 1955, this ratio was then raised to 90 per cent in 1965.[11]

ECONOMIC EFFECTS OF EXCHANGE-CONTROL LIBERALIZATION

In undertaking the decontrol efforts between 1960 and 1965 the main objectives of the government were to satisfy the persistent demands of exporters for a more favorable exchange rate and, by relying more on free-market forces, to meet charges of favoritism and poor administration in allocating foreign exchange. There was no intent to bring about a significant contraction in the industrial sector, where development had been fostered by exchange controls. It is for this reason that decontrol measures were coupled with such actions as tariff increases, the extension of especially favorable credit terms to certain industries, and the granting of tax exemptions to so-called basic industries. The discriminatory sales taxes and the highly protectionist tariff system, which became effective as quantitative controls were eliminated, also did much to continue the sheltering of domestic industry from foreign competition. In short, exchange controls were removed, but liberalization in the sense of a significant easing of all controls over imports did not occur.

Import Prices and Quantities.

From 1959 to 1962, when the exchange rate per dollar including the margin fee rose from P2.50 to P3.90, or by 56 per cent, the wholesale price index of imported products increased only 22 per cent. If the rise in the dollar price of imports is taken into account, the net rise in import prices associated with the increase in the price of foreign exchange was only 15 per cent. In view of the very high windfall profits that had existed on most imported goods, this much smaller rise in the peso prices of imported goods compared with the peso price of a dollar is not surprising. Permitting unlimited imports of most items at the same time that the currency was depreciated meant that these windfall gains absorbed most of the price-increasing effects of the depreciation.[12]

Further information on price behavior can be obtained by grouping the imported goods included in the wholesale price index according to exchange control classes. Classifying on this basis indicates the following price rises from 1959 to 1962: essential consumer goods, 46 per cent; essential producer goods, 20 per cent; semiessential producer goods, 11 per cent; and nonessential consumer goods, 9 per cent.[13] The higher price rise for more essential goods conforms to what would be expected, since these were already being imported quite liberally in 1959, and importers did not, therefore, reap large windfall gains. Thus, a larger share of the increased peso cost of foreign goods had to be passed on to wholesalers.[14]

This larger price rise in essential goods also meant, of course, that the decontrol efforts were successful in narrowing somewhat the differences in the degree of protection among nonessential consumer goods, essential producer goods, and essential consumer goods. In 1959 the price indices (1949 = 100) for nonessential consumer goods and essential producer goods were 2.25 and 1.25 times higher, respectively, than the price index for essential consumer goods. In 1962 these ratios were only 1.69 and 1.03. However, decontrol was only a partial effort toward equalizing incentives among manufacturing sectors. Removing the windfall gains associated with exchange controls still left the highly protective system that resulted from the 1957 Tariff Code and the discriminatory system of sales taxes. Furthermore, as noted earlier, tariff rates for many import-substitution industries were sharply raised at the time of the 1962 exchange-rate depreciation. The explicit tariff rate for a sample of nonessential consumer goods analyzed by Valdepeñas increased from 51 per cent in 1957 to 83 per cent in the 1962–67 period.[15] Import duties on essential consumer goods rose from 18 to 38 per cent in the same period; producer goods, from 25 to 47 per cent.

Some information on the behavior of import quantities during the decontrol episode can be obtained by grouping imports according to exchange-control categories and then constructing quantity indices for these categories. However, because of the well-known serious deficiencies with unit values even at the most detailed level at which import statistics are reported, the results of this exercise must be regarded with some skepticism. They show the following percentage changes in import quantities between 1959 and 1962: essential consumer goods, −13.0; essential producer goods, −3.0; semiessential producer goods, −18.0; and nonessential consumer goods, +19.0.[16] The rise in imports of nonessential consumer goods relative to essential consumer and producer goods is what one would expect from the decontrol program unless there were offsetting tariff changes. Although tariffs on nonessential consumer goods were raised, apparently these increases were not enough to counter entirely the effect of easing the previously severe restrictions on importing nonessential consumer goods. Presumably the significant decline in imports of semiessential producer goods is related to the rise in imports of nonessential consumer goods, since the former set of goods are used in part to produce the latter goods domestically.

Manufacturing and Export Activities.

Many import-competing manufacturing activities were, of course, adversely affected by the liberalization because manufacturers who had directly imported raw materials and capital goods at the exchange rate of P2 to the dollar and thus had reaped the windfall gain themselves now were faced with higher input costs. Import prices of competitive final outputs also increased but by less than the price increase for imported producer goods. The average annual rate of growth in the manufacturing sector declined from 7.7 per cent between 1957 and 1959 (a rate already considerably less than that during the early 1950s) to 3.8 per cent from 1960 to 1962 and 3.7 per cent for the entire 1960–65 period. The unfavorable impact of decontrol on non-export-oriented manufacturing is confirmed by Castro's study of profit rates before and during the liberalization period.[17] His figures show that the ratio of net profits (after taxes) to total assets for manufacturing firms (excluding sugar mills, lumber and plywood, and cordage) fell from 11.8 per cent for 1957–59 to 6.4 per cent for 1960–62.

The main test of the success of a liberalization effort is whether or not resources are pulled into export activities. Export values did indeed rise significantly during the decontrol period (see Table 1-2 and Chart 1-1). From a level of about $550 million between 1959 and 1962, exports rose after the 1962 depreciation to around $750 million between 1963 and 1965. With the removal in 1965 of the penalty rate against exporters, the value again jumped in the next year to about $850 million. (In volume terms, the increase was 24 per cent between 1962 and 1963 and 6 per cent between 1965 and 1966.) As is pointed out in Chapter 5, Hicks has shown that there was considerable understatement of the value of exports between 1960 and 1962, whereas exports were slightly overvalued in 1963.[18] After 1965, declared export values again were too low. Thus, the export rise associated with the devaluation actually consisted more of a fairly steady increase between 1959 and 1966 than spectacular increases in a few years. After adjusting the declared value by Hicks's corrective factors, the increase in export values between these two years still turns out to be an impressive 57 per cent. Even deducting the $20 million increase in the value of sugar exports between 1959 and 1966, which was due to the U.S. quota increase, still gives a 53 per cent increase in the value of exports between these years.

The increase in the growth rate of exports covered manufactured as well as nonmanufactured commodities. Between 1956–61 and 1962–66 the average yearly growth rate of manufactured exports increased from 6.0 per cent to 7.9 per cent.[19] If traditional manufactured exports, namely, coconut oil and sugar, are excluded from these exports, the export growth rates for these two periods are 8.5 per cent and 14.6 per cent, respectively. Although these are impressive increases in growth rates, the rise between these periods in the growth rate for exports of nonmanufactured commodities was even larger.[20]

Not only was the shift in resources toward export activities reflected directly in the value of exports, but also in profit rates, savings, and levels of productive activity in the export sector. Castro found, for example, that in contrast to the decline for his sample of manufacturing firms, profit rates for mining corporations rose from 11.2 per cent for 1956–59 to 16.2 per cent for 1960–62. The corresponding rise for agricultural corporations was from 4.7 to 4.9 per cent.[21] Another manifestation of this shift in income is seen in the findings of Paauw and Tryon that, after a decade of dissaving, agricultural savings turned positive in 1961 and grew rapidly through 1964 (the last year for which they have data on savings).[22] The most significant shift in production in the agricultural sector occurred in the area devoted to commercial export crops and to food crops produced for domestic consumption. As Treadgold and Hooley point out in their excellent analysis of the redistributive effects of the decontrol effort, the proportions in which the supply of cultivatable land is divided between these two types of productive activities are quite responsive (with a time lag) to the relative prices of agricultural export products and agricultural products for home consumption.[23] Thus, when export prices (in pesos) rose relative to the prices of locally consumed foods during the early phases of the liberalization period, there was a sizable shift toward the production of export crops. Specifically, the harvested area of commercial crops, which had risen only about 3 per cent between 1955 and 1960, increased over 40 per cent from 1960 to 1965, whereas the harvested area of food crops increased nearly 30 per cent in the first period but remained unchanged in the second. Similarly, the output of commercial crops increased at an annual average rate of 1.9 per cent from 1955 to 1960 and 6.1 per cent annually from 1960 to 1965, in contrast to an annual rate for food output of 4.4 per cent in the 1955–60 period and 3.1 per cent in 1960–65.

Not only did the shift away from cultivating food crops in favor of export crops tend to cause a supply-induced rise in food prices, but the redistribution of income toward the rural sector tended to reinforce this rise from the demand side, since the expenditure elasticity in the Philippines for food products has been found to be 0.76 for rural families compared to only 0.41 for urban families.[24] The net effect of these forces was that the food component of the consumer price index rose 58 per cent between 1959 and 1965, most of the rise occurring in the second half of that period. The other components of the cost of living index increased by the following percentages between these years: clothing, 27; rent and repairs, 7; fuel, light, and water, 18; and miscellaneous items, 15. The rise in the composite index was 33 per cent.[25]

The rise in the absolute price level during the early 1960s was related to the easy credit policies pursued by the monetary authorities. As previously noted, the rediscount rate was cut from 6.5 per cent in 1959 to 3 per cent by 1961, and the reserve requirement for commercial banks was reduced from 21 per cent in 1959 to 15 per cent by 1961. The result was that the money supply increased at an annual average rate of nearly 16 per cent between 1960 and 1963 as compared to an annual average rate of only 6.5 per cent between 1953 and 1960.

The burden of the rise in food prices fell to a considerable extent upon industrial workers, since their money wage rates rose only modestly in response to increasing prices. From 1959 to 1964, money wage rates for skilled and unskilled workers rose 6 per cent, and for unskilled workers, 12 per cent, while the consumer price index increased 28 per cent. However, in 1965 an increase of 2 pesos per day in the minimum wage rate helped to restore part of the real wage loss for unskilled workers. Consequently, as of 1965 real wage rates for these workers were 8 per cent below the 1959 level.[26] Of course, the increase in money wages placed still further pressures, in addition to those resulting from the increased costs of imported inputs, on profit rates in the industrial sector.

Conclusions.

As mentioned at the outset of this section, the government dismantled exchange controls mainly because of the corruption and maladministration connected with them and the pressures of exporters for a more favorable exchange rate. President Macapagal took special care in his 1962 address on the state of the nation to inform the business community that the government, in removing controls, wished merely to substitute tariff protection for the protection provided by the control system.[27] Protection of domestic industry was in itself regarded as a legitimate and desirable goal. Consequently, the fact that the decontrol effort did not significantly reduce the size of the import-substitution sector built up during the period of quantitative controls is not surprising. Actually, what must have surprised government officials was the extent of the economic difficulties that the import-substitution sector did face. They did not seem to appreciate that, by providing the export sector with more favorable trading terms and increasing the import costs of raw materials and capital goods, resources would be pulled out of the new industrial sector even if the level of protection on final consumption goods was maintained. In a sense, the decontrol episode was partly successful in changing the production incentives built into the economy during the 1950s despite the intentions of the government. But the resulting situation was not very satisfactory from an economic standpoint, since a significant liberalization effort that could have established the basis for a new type of export-oriented growth was not achieved and the import-substituting manufacturing sector was left in a relatively stagnant state.

NOTES

1. This selling rate also applied to Philippine government purchases, reinsurance premiums, and existing contractual obligations previously approved by the Central Bank.

2. As before, unclassified items could not be purchased without specific authorization of the Central Bank. The extent of the depreciation was increased by transferring 29 items previously classified as essential producer goods as well as 67 items previously classified as semiessential producer goods to the category of nonessential producer goods.

3. At that time the preferential rates for loans secured by agricultural or industrial

paper declined from 4½ to 4 per cent, and for loans secured by export bills, from 5 to 4 per cent.

4. These included a wide array of textile items, certain sizes of corrugated roofing sheets and plain galvanized sheets, unsweetened chocolate, chewing gum, book cloth, certain types of raw or green coffee, Portland cement, and certain parts of radios and radio-phonograph combinations.

5. Some of the industries enumerated in the act as "basic industries" were basic iron, nickel, aluminum, and steel; basic chemicals; copper and aluminum smelting and refining; pulping and the integrated manufacture of paper products; refining of gold, silver, and other precious materials; mining and exploration of base metals and crude oil or petroleum; production of agricultural crops; logging and the manufacture of veneer and plywoods; vegetable oil manufacturing, processing, and refining; manufacture of irrigation equipment and farm machinery; production and manufacture of textiles, cotton, ramie, synthetic fibers, and coconut coir; and the manufacture of food products.

6. Vicente B. Valdepeñas, Jr., *The Protection and Development of Philippine Manufacturing* (Manila: Ateneo University Press, 1970), pp. 47–50.

7. Certain foreign-exchange obligations of the Central Bank also were amortized at the official rate.

8. The May circular also excluded raw materials imports by local industries from the special time-deposit requirement and permitted the financing of those goods not requiring time deposits by means of documents against payment and documents against acceptances not exceeding 90 days.

9. The financing of imports not covered by the time-deposit requirement was also extended from 90 to 120 days for producing importers (but not merchant importers), and open-account financing of raw materials by local industries was permitted for 120 days.

10. President Diosdado Macapagal, "Five-Year Integrated Socio-Economic Program for the Philippines," in *A Stone for the Edifice: Memoirs of a President* (Quezon City: Mac, 1968).

11. In 1964 local manufacturers of phonographs, combination radio and phonograph sets, television sets, and combination radio and television sets were also granted the same type of tax preference given local manufacturers of refrigerating equipment in 1961. Specifically, the sales or compensating tax for domestically manufactured items in this group was reduced to 7 per cent, while the tax on imports was still held at 45 per cent.

12. It is theoretically possible for import prices either to rise or fall when a currency is depreciated and exchange controls are abandoned.

13. Table 5-6 contains price information for these groups of commodities from 1951 to 1970.

14. The tariff increases on imported nonessential consumer goods also acted to absorb part of the windfall gains earned on luxury imports and therefore had the effect of requiring part of the increased peso costs of importing to be passed on in the form of higher prices. However, these tariff increases were not sufficient to raise wholesale prices for imported nonessential consumer goods as much as for imported essential items.

15. Valdepeñas, *Philippine Manufacturing*, p. 81.

16. The number of items included in the indices are 9 for essential consumer goods, 42 for essential producer goods, 14 for semiessential producer goods, and 26 for nonessential consumer goods. Unit values for 1962 were used as weights for the various quantities.

17. Amado A. Castro, "Philippine Export Performance," in T. Morgan and

N. Spoelstra, eds., *Economic Interdependence in Southeast Asia* (Madison: University of Wisconsin Press, 1969), pp. 189–192.

18. George L. Hicks, "Philippine Foreign Trade, 1950–1965: Basic Data and Major Characteristics" and "Supplementary Data and Interpretations, 1954–1966" (Washington, D.C.: National Planning Association, Center for Development Planning, 1967; mimeo.).

19. Gerardo P. Sicat, *Economic Policy and Philippine Development* (Quezon City: University of Philippines Press, 1972), p. 69.

20. Ibid., p. 71.

21. Castro, "Philippine Export Performance," p. 190.

22. Douglas S. Paauw and Joseph L. Tryon, "Agriculture-Industry Interrelationships in an Open Dualistic Economy: The Philippines, 1949–1964," in "Growth of Output in the Philippines" (Papers presented at a conference of the International Rice Research Institute, Los Baños, Laguna, December 9–10, 1966; mimeo.), pp. 7–34 and Table X.

23. M. Treadgold and R. W. Hooley, "Decontrol and the Reduction of Income Flows: A Second Look," *Philippine Economic Journal*, Second Semester 1967, pp. 109–128.

24. From an unpublished study by J. Williamson and A. Kelley.

25. For a more detailed analysis of the manner in which various items on the index behaved as well as for a general discussion of the food inflation, see A. C. Ross, "Understanding the Philippine Inflation," *Philippine Economic Journal*, Second Semester 1966, pp. 228–259.

26. The increase in the minimum wage also probably increased unemployment among unskilled workers.

27. Macapagal, *Five-Year Program*, p. 21.

Chapter 4

Renewed Economic Expansion and New Balance-of-Payments Problems, 1966–71

THE FIRST MARCOS ADMINISTRATION, 1966–69

Expansionary Monetary and Fiscal Policies, 1966 to Mid-1967.

Immediately upon its assumption of power in 1966, the Marcos administration initiated vigorous efforts to accelerate development in both the agricultural and industrial sectors. In the first month of the year, the monetary authorities pursued a policy which they described as one "of massive credit relaxation." [1] The basic rediscount rate of 6 per cent was lowered to 4¾ per cent, rediscount ceilings on commercial banks were raised, reserve requirements against savings and time deposits were reduced, and the reserve requirement on special time deposits was cut from 100 per cent to 50 per cent.

Further steps to ease the credit situation followed in later months. The reserve requirement on special time deposits was reduced to 25 per cent in February, and finally in March the special time-deposit requirement for all import letters of credit and the reserve requirement against these deposits were eliminated. With this policy step the exchange-control system became completely liberalized. (However, Phase V of the Bhagwati-Krueger schema is dated as beginning in November 1965, when a unified exchange rate was established.) Rediscount ceilings continued to be increased with the result that by July 1966 the amount of Central Bank credit available to the commercial banks was three times as large as that available in December 1965. Special advances from the Central Bank outside of the rediscount ceilings were also made available to certain banks. In June, the old selective credit system establishing credit ceilings for different types of loans was abolished and replaced by a more modest scheme limiting the types of credit instruments eligible for rediscounting at the Central Bank.

The monetary authorities continued their easy money policy through the first half of 1967. For example, in support of the government's efforts to expand rice production, the Central Bank in early 1967 issued circulars permitting commercial banks to rediscount a larger proportion of the commercial paper issued by the Rice and Corn Administration (RCA) and authorizing the Philippine National Bank to rediscount promissory notes of the RCA with the Central Bank at the 3 per cent preferred rate. The regulations covering foreign borrowing through standby letters of credit for the purpose of generating pesos were also eased. Still another expansionary policy was the reduction of the maximum interest rate paid on time deposits by commercial and savings banks from 6½ per cent to 6 per cent. The announced purpose of this move was to enable these banks to reduce their prime rates on loans for production purposes and for projects included in the government's development program.

Another important financial operation aimed at restoring full utilization of the economy's productive capacity was the so-called rehabilitation program of the Development Bank of the Philippines (DBP). This refinancing program for distressed firms consisted of three parts, namely: (1) refinancing through such conventional methods as loan extensions, deferments, and revision of loan terms; (2) conversion of DBP industrial loan accounts into preferred stock of the assisted firms which later could be converted into common stock; (3) foreign-exchange financing of imports of machinery and raw materials through credit lines and guarantees arranged by DBP with banking institutions and government export-import agencies abroad. Between April 1966, when the program started, and the end of the year, about fifteen hundred loan accounts amounting to P252 million were refinanced through conventional methods, whereas a total of P62 million was invested by the bank in the preferred stock of some eight firms. In 1967, refinancing through conventional methods totaled P265 million and through the securities scheme P735 million. To implement the refinancing program, the bank issued bonds that could, if the holder wished, later be exchanged for any of the industrial preferred shares available in the bank's portfolio. By the end of 1967, about P200 million worth of such bonds had been issued.

In addition to providing easier credit conditions, the new administration embarked upon a large-scale program of economic development which emphasized rural infrastructure investments such as roads, irrigation projects, schools, telecommunications, etc. The administration apparently chose to focus upon rural development on the grounds that it was the rural sector which was constraining efforts to restore the high growth rates of the 1950s.

In particular, the most influential economic advisers of that time believed that the inflation of about 25 per cent in food prices between 1962 and 1965 was the major factor in preventing the earlier decontrol and currency depreciation efforts from restoring high growth rates. Expanding the rural growth rate would supposedly provide larger amounts of foreign exchange for imports of capital goods and raw materials by increasing traditional exports and reducing food imports, would increase the supplies of wage goods for the industrial sector, and would increase the market for domestic manufactures. The magnitude and composition of the national government's capital expenditures program from 1959 through 1971 are indicated in Table 4-1. As is shown in the table, the volume of capital outlays rose significantly in the 1966–69 period. However, distribution of expenditures between social and economic development remained essentially unchanged.

In order to finance capital formation activities of the national and local governments as well as those of such government corporations as the Development Bank of the Philippines, and also provide funds for expanded current expenditures on developmental services, it was necessary for the government to engage in extensive borrowing both internally and externally (see Table 4-2). The internal debt increased from P3.1 billion at the end of 1965, or 14.7 per cent of GNP, to P5.8 billion by the end of 1969, or 18.4 per cent of GNP; and the external public debt rose from $491 million to $828 million between these years. The Central Bank, the commercial banks, and various government entities ended up as the main holders of outstanding internal debt. Specifically, about P2.4 million of the P2.7 million total increase in internal debt was absorbed by these institutions.

Credit Tightening and the Reintroduction of Exchange Controls, Mid-1967 Through 1968.

The significant expansion of domestic credit and the rise in government investment expenditures brought about an upward movement in prices as well as a deterioration in the balance of trade. Wholesale prices rose 6.6 per cent between 1965 and 1966 and 7.4 per cent between 1966 and 1967. However, more important to policymakers than the price rise was the worsening of the country's trade balance. From a trade account surplus of $24 million in 1965 and a deficit of $9 million in 1966, the merchandise trade deficit rose to $224 million in 1967. To help finance these additional net imports, the country drew on its gold tranche of $27.5 million at the International Monetary Fund. Other important policies that were undertaken by the Central Bank in the period from mid-1967 through 1968 are summarized in Table 4-3.

Starting in mid-1967, the Central Bank began to reverse its easy credit policies. In June of that year, the bank acted to raise the reserve requirements

TABLE 4-1

Average Annual Capital Outlays[a] by the National Government and Ratio of Total Government Expenditures to GNP, Fiscal Years, 1959–71

(values in millions of pesos)

	1959–61		1962–65		1966–69		1970–71	
	Value	Percentage Distribution	Value	Percentage Distribution	Value	Percentage Distribution	Value	Percentage Distribution
Economic development	189.5	76.4	254.6	85.3	370.8	84.9	463.1	82.5
Agriculture and natural resources	49.3	20.6	83.2	27.9	79.4	18.2	70.6	12.6
Transport and communications	102.5	42.0	147.2	49.3	215.2	49.3	255.7	45.6
Commerce and industry	15.9	5.0	7.7	2.6	4.4	1.01	37.2	6.6
Other	21.8	8.8	16.5	5.5	71.8	16.4	99.6	17.7
Social development	45.5	18.1	33.1	11.1	45.6	10.4	69.1	12.3
Education	26.0	10.7	15.2	5.1	36.8	8.4	50.1	8.9
Public health and medical care	17.8	6.9	13.1	4.4	8.2	1.9	14.5	2.6
Labor and welfare	1.6	0.5	4.8	1.6	0.6	0.1	4.4	0.8
National defense	2.7	1.2	2.1	0.7	6.0	1.4	11.4	2.0
General government	9.9	4.2	8.7	2.9	14.2	3.3	17.6	3.1
Total	247.5	100.0	298.5	100.0	436.6	100.0	561.2	100.0
Ratio: total government expenditures to GNP[b]	10.50%		11.16%		11.12%		12.48%	

SOURCE: Philippine Budget Commission.

a. Data on capital outlays are for fiscal years.

b. Data on total government expenditures and GNP are for calendar years.

TABLE 4-2

**Internal and External Debt of the Government
and Monetary Institutions, 1949–71**

End-of-year Averages	Internal Debt (millions of pesos)				External Debt (millions of dollars)		
	Total	National Govt.	Local Govt.	Govt. Corp.	Total	Govt.	Monetary Institutions
1949	466	317	66	83	117	117	—
1950–53	666	503	65	98	111	111	—
1954–57	1,266	915	40	311	89	89	—
1958–61	2,136	1,465	32	639	175	139	35
1962–65	2,904	1,831	35	1,038	324	219	105
1966–69	4,522	2,686	102	1,734	689	359	330
1970–71	6,635	3,966	106	2,534	1,058	556	502

SOURCE: Central Bank of the Philippines, *Statistical Bulletin*, December, 1970, pp. 251–252 and 256; and Central Bank, *Annual Report*, 1971, pp. 26 and 29.

TABLE 4-3

Major Trade, Payments, and Related Economic Policies, 1967–68

June 1967	Central Bank initiated stage-by-stage increase in reserve requirements from 12 to 16 per cent; raised rediscount rate from 4¾ to 6 per cent, and required commercial banks to maintain 1-to-1 ratio between actual foreign-exchange assets and foreign-exchange liabilities.
	Reimposition of cash margin deposits when letters of credit are opened.
Feb. 1968	Further increase in rediscount rate to 7.5 per cent.
March 1968	Imposition of absolute limit on foreign-exchange liabilities of commercial banks.
June 1968	Replacement of cash margin requirement with special time-deposit requirement against letters of credit: the less essential the imported goods, the higher the percentage requirement.
Oct. 1968	Imposition on commercial banks of ceilings on domestic loans and on foreign-currency letters of credit.
	Announcement of stage-by-stage reduction in time-deposit requirement against letters of credit for essential producer goods. Imposition of ceilings on credit for import financing and on domestic loan portfolios.

for commercial banks gradually from 12 per cent to 16 per cent, increased the basic rediscount rate from 4¾ per cent to 6 per cent, stipulated that commercial banks must maintain a 1-to-1 ratio between actual foreign-exchange assets and foreign-exchange liabilities, and issued a circular under which all imports over $100 were to be covered by letters of credit. Furthermore, the monetary authorities were successful, through so-called moral suasion, in obtaining an agreement among the commercial banks to impose cash margin deposits on the opening of letters of credit. The schedule was as follows:

Essential producer and consumer goods	25%
Semiessential producer goods	50
Semiessential consumer and nonessential producer goods	75
Luxury items and nonessential consumer goods and others	150

The margin deposits were subject to a 100 per cent reserve, 50 per cent of which could be in the form of government securities. The deposits were to be held by the banks until the corresponding import bills were liquidated. Together with other controls imposed during the 1967–70 period over the free use of foreign exchange, this action marked a return of the Philippines to Phase I of the Bhagwati-Krueger schema, namely, the introduction and gradual tightening of exchange controls. However, it must be emphasized that these controls were much less stringent than those adopted in the early 1950s. Later in 1967, exemptions from the margin requirement were made for certain raw materials imported by selected local industries, for some 57 commodities in the essential-consumer-goods category, and for 4 items in the essential-producer-goods category. Furthermore, the financing of imports of these items was permitted through open-account arrangements.

Two later actions involved accelerating the increase in the reserve requirement against demand deposits so that it reached 16 per cent by November 30, 1967, and restricting the sale of foreign exchange for travel to $50 per person per day with a yearly maximum of $1,500 per person.

Additional steps to limit credit and reduce the drain on foreign exchange continued to be adopted in 1968. In February the basic rediscount rate was raised from 6 per cent to 7½ per cent, and the preferential rate for loans on rice and corn, from 3 per cent to 4 per cent. In the international area, the Central Bank, in March 1968, lifted the requirement that commercial banks maintain a full cover of their foreign-exchange liabilities, but introduced in its place a requirement that, for any one bank, foreign-exchange liabilities not exceed their June 27, 1967, level or $1.5 million, whichever was higher. However, in September, this was raised to $2.5 million per bank. To increase the time during which the cash margin must be held, the Central Bank also stipulated, in March, that letters of credit must be opened on or before the actual date of shipment.

In June 1968 the cash margin requirement was replaced by a special time-deposit requirement against letters of credit, which were to be held for 120 days. The percentages were also increased to the following levels:

Essential producer and consumer goods	50%
Semiessential producer goods	75
Nonessential producer and semiessential consumer goods	100
Nonessential consumer goods and unclassified items	175

In October the time-deposit requirement for essential producer goods was modified: it was immediately reduced to 40 per cent and then was reduced gradually to a level of 25 per cent by mid-December. A few additional changes in the other groups of items were also made. As a result, by mid-December the rates were as follows:[2]

Essential producer goods	25%
Essential consumer goods	50
Semiessential producer goods	75
Nonessential producer and semiessential consumer goods	100
Semiunclassified producer goods	125
Nonessential consumer and semiunclassified consumer goods	150
Unclassified producer and unclassified consumer goods	175

In order to prevent the October reduction of the special time deposit for essential producer goods from aggravating the deficit pressures on the balance of payments, the Central Bank simultaneously imposed ceilings on credits for import financing as well as on domestic loan portfolios. As of mid-November 1968, total outstanding foreign-currency letters of credits and total credits for import financing were limited to their mid-October levels. However, imports for dollar-earning industries or infrastructure projects, including the government's development program, were exempted from the ceilings. The ceiling set on banks' domestic loan portfolios was 105 per cent of the level of these portfolios as of October 12, 1968, and was reduced to 102 per cent of that level on December 31. Export credits as well as loans for rice and corn production or distribution were exempted from this requirement.

Despite tightened credit policies and the introduction of controls over foreign-exchange dealings, domestic loans and investments by the banking system expanded 21 per cent in 1967 and another 11 per cent in 1968. The time-deposit requirement was not as effective as was hoped for, due to foreign financing of the special time deposit.[3] The trade account deficit rose from its 1967 level of $224 million to $274 million in 1968. Again the Central Bank resorted to assistance from the IMF and drew on its first and second credit tranche totaling $55 million.

One encouraging factor in the country's growth efforts in 1968 was the relative stability of prices. Despite the 11 per cent increase in domestic credits, wholesale prices rose only 4.8 per cent, and consumer prices, 0.7 per cent. The major reason for this reasonably satisfactory price performance was the breakthrough in rice production starting in the latter part of 1967. The successful use of high-yielding varieties of rice as well as the expansion of irrigation facilities not only increased yields per acre by 4.4 per cent between 1967 and 1968 but also led to a 6.7 per cent increase in the harvest area for rice. Between 1960 and 1966 total rice production had risen only 9 per cent, whereas between 1966 and 1968 it increased 18 per cent.

Balance-of-Payments Difficulties in 1969.

The balance-of-payments situation continued to worsen as the government pursued deficit-spending activities, until it reached crisis proportions near the end of 1969. The major actions of the Central Bank in that year are indicated in Table 4-4. During the first few months of the year, controls over

TABLE 4-4

Major Trade, Payments, and Related Economic Policies, 1969

April 1969	Reduction in length of period that special time deposits must be held, and exclusion of domestic loans to certain export industries from previously instituted credit ceilings.
	Lifting of ceiling on foreign-exchange liabilities of commercial banks.
	Increase in rediscount rate from 7.5 to 8.0 per cent.
June 1969	Introduction of 2 per cent levy on all Central Bank loans and advances. Loans to government and high-priority export industries were excluded from this charge.
	Opening of import letters of credit permitted only for essential consumer and producer goods, semiessential producer goods, and nonessential producer goods. Ceiling for permitted letters of credit in these categories also reduced.
Nov. 1969	Further reduction in ceiling on import letters of credit.

trade were actually eased somewhat, though the trade deficit for the first two quarters was running at an annual rate of $270 million. In April, for example, the Central Bank reduced the period during which banks must hold the special time deposits required for import letters of credit from 120 days to 90 days for the following groups of commodities: essential producer goods; essential consumer goods; semiessential producer goods; semiessential consumer goods;

nonessential producer goods; and semiunclassified producer goods. For the four remaining categories—nonessential consumer goods, semiunclassified consumer goods, unclassified producer goods, and unclassified consumer goods—the time requirement remained at 120 days. The bank also issued a memorandum, in April, excluding export-oriented industries from the ceilings on domestic loans.[4] Imports of machinery and equipment for use in export-oriented activities were also exempted from the special time-deposit requirement.[5]

Additional liberalizing measures were taken in April 1969. Most important was the lifting of the ceiling on foreign-exchange liabilities of commercial banks. Another was the revoking of a November 1968 circular of the Central Bank requiring currency declarations for departing and returning Philippine residents, while still another was the granting of permission for 100 per cent of the reserves against special time deposits to consist of government securities.

At the same time that particular industries and activities were given special incentives to expand production, there were also some efforts to curtail expansionary forces on a general level. For example, the rediscount rate was increased in April from 7½ per cent to 8 per cent. In June, an additional charge of 2 per cent was levied on all Central Bank loans and advances. Thus, in effect, the rediscount rate was increased to 10 per cent. The reason given by the Central Bank for the levy was to align its rates with those prevailing in world money markets. As has been the practice after the introduction of strong restrictive measures by the Central Bank, exceptions to the 2 per cent interest charge soon appeared, including loans and advances to the government, loans to commercial banks secured by government securities and promissory notes of the Rice and Corn Administration. High-priority export activities were also excluded from the 2 per cent levy.

As is typical of the seasonal pattern in receipts and payments, during the first seven months of the year government receipts were slightly larger than disbursements. This surplus was, however, much too small to offset the large budget deficit of the last five months that was related to the presidential election in November. The net deficit for the year was P934 million—an amount over three times larger than in the previous year and roughly equal to the cumulative deficits between 1961 and 1968. Equally dramatic was the 20 per cent rise in the money supply in the last four months of 1969—from P4.0 million in August to P4.8 million in December. Of course, the large deficit and large increase in the money supply were closely related. Central Bank loans to the national government together with securities of the national government held by the Central Bank rose by P445 million in the last six months, and national-government securities held by commercial banks increased by P219 million in the same time period.

The growing destabilizing effects of the monetary and fiscal developments in the last part of the year forced the Central Bank to adopt highly restrictive policies toward the private sector. As of June 18, 1969, import letters of credit could be opened only for four categories of commodities, namely, essential producer goods, essential consumer goods, semiessential producer goods, and nonessential producer goods. Furthermore, for the four permitted types of imports a 15 per cent cutback was imposed, on June 18, on import letters of credit relative to their October 1968–March 1969 levels, and another 15 per cent was added on July 15. The level of 70 per cent of the base was held until November, when the ceiling was further restricted to 55 per cent of the base period, and the opening of letters of credit was divided into weekly allotments. For all imports other than those in the four categories mentioned, the Central Bank stipulated that its prior authorization was required.[6] Still another restrictive measure taken in November was to remove the privilege of open-account financing on imports of certain essential consumer and producer goods. These were made subject to the general rule that imports must be financed by letters of credit. Regulations on nonmerchandise trade were also tightened.[7]

One indication of the seriousness of the financial situation near the end of 1969 was that the Central Bank was forced to assume the interest burden on the foreign credit lines of the Philippine National Bank (PNB) that were associated with overdrafts of the PNB's accounts with certain U.S. commercial banks. In addition, from December until the peso was floated on February 21, 1970, there were no interbank foreign-exchange transactions, since commercial banks were required to surrender to the Central Bank foreign-exchange holdings in excess of 25 per cent of outstanding foreign-currency liabilities.

The 1966–69 period demonstrates that Philippine economic development cannot long be sustained at a high rate unless there is also a high growth rate of export earnings. Extensive credit creation and foreign borrowing can initiate periods of prosperity; but unless these measures are accompanied by exchange-rate policies designed to maintain a vigorous export sector, these periods of expanding economic activity are doomed to end suddenly as balance-of-payments problems eventually build up to a crisis.

Export Incentives.

One merit of the development efforts of the Marcos administration was the greater attention paid to expanding exports, especially of industrial products, than in previous administrations. Some of the special treatment given to export activities has already been pointed out. The Investment Incentives Act of 1967, which was aimed at stimulating production in key domestic industries as well as in export activities, is another example of this concern for increasing exports. Under the act, a Board of Investment (BOI) was established which determines the industries that qualify for special aid. Firms are registered as either "preferred" or "pioneer," the latter being those that produce new products or processes in the economy. The BOI determines the list of activities that fit these two categories of investment. The main forms of assistance to registered firms are: (1) exemption for seven years from import duties and compensating taxes on imports of capital goods or a tax credit equivalent to these taxes if the capital goods are purchased from domestic firms, (2) deduction from taxable income of all capitalized preoperating expenses, (3) accelerated depreciation of fixed assets, (4) liberal carry-over features for operating losses, and (5) deduction from taxable income of reinvested earnings. In addition to these forms of assistance, pioneer firms are exempted from paying a certain proportion (which declines over time) of all national taxes except the income tax[8] and are given special tariff protection against competing imports. In pioneer industries, 100 per cent foreign ownership is permitted unless specifically prohibited by law. However, in preferred investment areas, only firms at least 60 per cent owned by Filipinos can obtain the special privileges until three years have expired after the industry has been designated a "preferred" area of investment. If Filipinos do not enter the industry within this time period, the nationality criterion is dropped.

Registered firms that export completely finished products receive, in addition to the aids previously cited, the following tax advantages: (1) double deduction from taxable income of export-promotion expenses, (2) double deduction from taxable income of freight costs incurred in connection with exporting if Philippine ships are used or a one and one-half deduction if foreign ships are employed, and (3) a tax credit equivalent to 7 per cent of the cost of raw materials used in export production.

The Export Incentives Act of 1970 expands the aids to export firms (defined as firms with at least 50 per cent of their sales to foreign countries) in the form of: (1) a tax credit equivalent to all sales, specific, and import taxes on the raw materials and supplies used in export production, replacing item 3 above; (2) a deduction of part of the firm's export revenue from taxable items for five years; and (3) an exemption from export taxes. Under item 2 just above, taxable income can be reduced for five years by the product of the proportion of direct labor costs in total costs, the proportion of local raw materials in total costs, the number 5, and export sales.[9]

THE 1970 EXCHANGE CRISIS AND ITS AFTERMATH

Exchange-Rate Policies in 1970 and 1971.

During January and most of February 1970, the government continued its policy of sharing the responsibility for rationing the limited supply of foreign exchange with the commercial banks. The ceilings for these banks on foreign-currency letters of credit, which had been reduced in November 1969 to 55 per cent of their base-period level, were renewed at these low levels in early January, as were the special time-deposit requirements for letters of credit. Moreover, reserve requirements for commercial banks, savings banks, development banks, and rural banks were all raised two percentage points in late January. This changed the reserve requirement for commercial banks from 16 per cent to 18 per cent by March.

The balance-of-payments situation continued to worsen, however. President Marcos underscored the seriousness of the problem when he told a business group in early January: "We have unfortunately financed the foreign-exchange requirements of our development with credits of short maturities. I am told by my advisers that because of the increase in short-term debts, the total payment for interest and amortization of foreign obligations of the country this fiscal year ending June 30 will take over one-half of our export earning." [10] More specifically, outstanding public and private foreign debts amounted to more than $1.6 billion by the end of 1969, of which over $450 million was due in 1970 and two-thirds within four years. Of the debt maturing in one year, $196 million was owed by the Central Bank, $58 million by the government, and $198 million by the private sector. [11]

The only realistic method of coping with the exchange crisis was again to request financial assistance from the International Monetary Fund and to ask foreign banks to agree to longer repayment terms. An IMF consultative group arrived in the Philippines on January 10, 1970. Foreign creditors took the position that they would accept a restructuring of their debt provided the government agreed to the IMF's stabilization recommendations for correcting the country's weak financial condition and thereby obtained its third credit tranche from the fund. [12] The advice of the fund on exchange-rate policy was either to devalue significantly or float the peso.

The government chose to float the peso rather than devalue sharply, and freed the peso on February 21, 1970. This action together with the other major policies followed in 1970 and 1971 are summarized in Table 4-5. The peso-dollar rate promptly rose, from P3.90 to over P5.5, and reached P6.4 by the end of the year. At the same time that the exchange rate was permitted to move to its free-market level, the Central Bank lifted the monthly ceilings on foreign-currency letters of credit, the special time-deposit requirement, and the ban on open-account financing arrangements. Certain exchange controls remained, however. The sale of foreign exchange for imports of non-essential consumer goods still required prior approval of the Central Bank. This prior-approval requirement in effect continued the ban on imports of some 400 luxury commodities. [13] Importation by means of documents against acceptances and open-account arrangements were permitted only for periods

TABLE 4-5

Major Trade, Payments, and Related Economic Policies, 1970–71

Feb. 1970	Peso floated in foreign-exchange markets, and peso-to-dollar rate rose to P6.4 by end of year. Some exchange controls removed but exporters of major products required to convert 80 per cent of their receipts at old rate of P3.90 per dollar.
	Special export tax of 8 or 10 per cent substituted for dual exchange-rate arrangement for exporters.
	Beginning of gradual two-percentage-point rise in reserve requirement for commercial banks.
July 1970	Issuance of circular requiring most imports to be covered by letters of credit. Commercial banks voluntarily accept 30 per cent (later raised to 50 per cent) margin deposit against letters of credit.
Nov. 1970	Passage of law limiting power of the government to borrow abroad.
Aug. 1971	Central Bank imposes 15 per cent reserve requirement against margin deposit required for letters of credit.
Nov. 1971	Reserve requirement on margin deposit against letters of credit raised to 50 per cent.

not shorter than 180 days. Ceilings and limitations on the sale of foreign exchange for current invisible payments such as travel abroad and remittances of profits also continued in operation. Furthermore, the explicit approval of the Central Bank was necessary for new foreign borrowings and investments, and the remittance of the assets of emigrants was restricted.

An important feature of the new exchange system for exporters was that 80 per cent of all receipts from the leading export products, namely, logs, centrifugal sugar, copra, and copper ores and concentrates were to be surrendered to the Central Bank at the old rate of P3.90 to the dollar. The remaining 20 per cent could be sold at the free-market rate. However, in May 1970, as a result of the strong opposition of exporters, a special stabilization tax on exports was substituted for this differential exchange-rate arrangement. For logs, copra, sugar, and copper ores and concentrates, the tax on the total value of exports was set at 10 per cent. An 8 per cent tax rate was established for the following exports: molasses, coconut oil, desiccated coconut meal or cake, unmanufactured abaca, unmanufactured tobacco, veneer core and sheets, plywood, lumber, canned pineapple, and bunker fuel oil. In addition, any product whose annual export value exceeded $5 million was made subject to the 8 per cent tax during the fiscal year following attainment of this export value. However, exceptions to the stabilization tax were also made. In July

1970, exports of pineapple juice and concentrates were exempted from the tax; and shortly thereafter refined sugar, wood moldings, diesel fuel oil, and industrial fuel oil were added to the exemption list.

Another aspect of the government's stabilization efforts was the establishment by the Central Bank in July of an Exchange Stabilization Fund. Commercial banks were required to sell 10 per cent of their foreign exchange receipts directly to the Central Bank in order to provide foreign exchange for the stabilization fund. The proceeds were used to fund deposits being maintained with the consortium of creditor commercial banks in the United States.

The peso cost of a dollar remained essentially unchanged at about P6.4 throughout 1971. Controls over the ability of importers to purchase certain imports continued in effect, but there was an easing of controls for export-oriented firms and firms registered with the Board of Investment (BOI). In February, for example, export-oriented firms were permitted to import machinery and equipment by means of documents against acceptance and open-account arrangements without prior Central Bank approval, provided payment was made within 360 days. This privilege was extended, in August, to BOI-registered firms as well as to importers purchasing agricultural machinery and equipment.[14]

Some restrictive measures were put into effect, however, in the last half of the year to limit imports and neutralize excess liquidity. In late July, for example, the Central Bank issued a circular requiring all imports to be covered by letters of credit except imports by firms with a history of open-account or document-against-acceptance arrangements.

Monetary and Fiscal Policies.

In addition to permitting the peso to depreciate, the government followed a policy of monetary and fiscal restraint as part of its stabilization program. Starting on May 1, 1970, reserve requirements were raised another 2 per cent in four successive equal monthly installments of one-half per cent, with the result that by August the requirement for commercial banks was 20 per cent. Rediscounting privileges were also curtailed.[15] Other anti-inflationary steps taken at this time were to rescind all previously granted exemptions on the 2 per cent interest equalization charge imposed by the Central Bank and to increase the maximum rate of interest that banks could pay on time deposits. An important voluntary measure agreed upon later in the year by the commercial banks was the adoption of a uniform minimum margin deposit against letters of credit. The level was initially set, in July, at 30 per cent, but was raised to 50 per cent in October 1970.

During 1971, the Central Bank continued trying to exercise monetary restraint. For example, it raised the preferred rediscount rate to all rural banks for certain paper from 2 per cent to 3 per cent and also established ceilings for credit accommodations by banks to their directors, officers, or principal stockholders. Firms that were delinquent in paying off debts to government financial institutions also were required to obtain the explicit consent of the Central Bank to obtain foreign exchange. The most important policy adopted by the Central Bank, however, was the imposition in August 1971 of a 15 per cent reserve requirement on commercial banks against the 50 per cent margin deposit required for letters of credit. In late November, after some postponements, the required reserve was raised to 30 per cent.

For most of 1970 the monetary authorities succeeded in halting any further increases in the money supply and were even able to decrease it for a time. However, by November the money supply had passed its January level and in December was 6.2 per cent above the December 1969 figure. The rise continued into 1971, with the result that the money supply as of December 1971 was 10.3 per cent greater than its December 1970 level.

The national government managed to achieve a surplus of P143 million in its operational cash transactions in 1970, but it incurred a deficit of P91 million in 1971. Both the internal and external public debt also increased over these two periods. The internal debt rose 8 per cent in 1970, mainly due to a net increase in Treasury bills and the issuance of new bonds for infrastructure investments by the various development corporations of the government. During 1971 the internal debt expanded another 10 per cent as an intensification of spending on infrastructure and social services took place.

Much of the increase in the external debt of the government and the monetary institutions from $828 million in December 1969 to $1,041 million in December 1970 (a 25 per cent increase) was related to the need for adequate working balances of foreign exchange after the exchange crises of late 1969. At the time that the peso was floated, the Central Bank obtained its third credit tranche of $27.5 million from the IMF, a $40 million credit from the Federal Reserve Bank of New York, a $40 million loan from the First National City Bank of New York, and $18.5 million under the country's special drawing rights at the IMF. Later in 1970 the Central Bank secured credits of $35 million from Japanese banks and $10 million from Manufacturers Hanover Trust of New York. Furthermore, in June the Central Bank successfully completed negotiations for the restructuring of $247 million of debt with U.S banks and $27 million with European banks. The U.S. debt, most of which had been due in 1970, was consolidated into a loan payable over a six-year period. After repayments during the year, the level of the Central Bank's external debt on December 31, 1970, was $102 million higher than a year earlier, and the country's total external debt was $140 million higher. However, during 1971 the total external debt increased only $34 million, or 3 per cent.[16]

In an effort to prevent future episodes of excessive foreign borrowing by the government, limits on borrowing from abroad were imposed under a law (R.A. 6142) passed in November 1970. Under this law the government is permitted to borrow only $1 billion from abroad at a rate of not more than $250 million a year. The credits also must have a minimum of 10 years' maturity, and the interest paid must not exceed the rate charged by international financial institutions. It is further stipulated that government guarantees of foreign borrowing by other institutions may not exceed $500 million.

Besides the upper bound set to government borrowing under the act, it is stated that the payment of amortization and interest on the country's *total* external debt must not exceed 20 per cent of average foreign-exchange receipts over the preceding three years. To implement this provision, the Central Bank issued Circulars 315 and 316, in December 1970, establishing guidelines on foreign borrowings, i.e., any credit over 360 days. First, the Central Bank reiterated the requirement that foreign loans to the private sector must have its prior approval. Next, the bank established the following minimum repayment terms for loans of differing magnitudes: (a) loans of $250,000 or less should have a maturity of at least five years; (b) loans of between $250,000 and $500,000 should be repayable in no less than eight years; and (c) loans over $500,000 should have a maturity period of at least twelve years. However, applications for loans exceeding $500,000 with at least an eight-year maturity period inclusive of a three-year grace period on repayments of principal should be approved for export industries. Loans to overcrowded industries or to firms in arrears with government financial institutions were not to be approved by the Central Bank. Finally, it was stipulated in Circular 315 that the interest rates on foreign borrowings should not be more than 2 per cent above the prime rate of the lending country.

Both the law passed by Congress and the circulars issued by the Central Bank can only be justified as emergency measures. Tying the length of the repayment period to the size of a loan is, for example, a highly arbitrary and inefficient long-run method of preventing excessive foreign borrowing.

Economic Effects of the Currency Depreciation.

As is indicated in Table 4-6, the dollar price of the peso increased significantly immediately after it was permitted to seek its free-market level on February 21, 1970. The rate thereafter continued to rise gradually, and in December 1970 it was fixed by agreement among the commercial banks. There was a slight decline in August and September 1971, but by December 1971, the rate had returned to its December 1970 level.

The fear of further intensification of the social unrest that was triggered by price rises associated with the currency depreciation apparently accounts

TABLE 4-6

Foreign-Exchange Rates, 1970–71
(pesos per U.S. dollar)

1970	January	3.902		September	6.338
	February 1–20	3.906		October	6.402
	February 21–28	5.556		November	6.402
	March	6.057		December	6.402
	April	6.132	1971	January–July	6.402
	May	6.082		August	6.391
	June	6.173		September	6.379
	July	6.203		October–November	6.400
	August	6.238		December	6.402

SOURCE: Central Bank of the Philippines, *Central Bank News Digest*, 1970 and 1971.

for the decision to fix the dollar value of the peso. Since excess demand conditions developed soon after the peso was stabilized, bankers again began rationing foreign exchange among established customers. They also began bidding among themselves for exporters' dollars, using such devices as offering exporters lower lending rates than prevailed in the general market. Of course, in effect this depreciated the peso still further.

Exports quickly increased after the currency depreciation. Their value had remained at around $850 million from 1966 through 1969 but rose 24 per cent to $1,062 million in 1970. In volume terms, exports, which had actually fallen about 5 per cent between 1966 and 1969, rose 14 per cent between 1969 and 1970. These favorable performances in value and volume terms continued in 1971. The value of exports rose 5 per cent, to $1,122 million, while the volume of exports increased 13 per cent. The balance of trade also improved dramatically. Because of the government's policies of monetary and fiscal constraint as well as its continued controls over some foreign-exchange payments, the value of imports declined by over $40 million between 1969 and 1970. The deficit on the trade account fell from $276 million in 1969 to $28 million in 1970. In 1971, the result was not quite as satisfactory, as imports rose to $1,186 million, but the trade deficit was still only $64 million.

Among individual items, coconut products exhibited an especially impressive export performance over the two-year period, 1970–71. The export quantities of these products from 1969 to 1971 rose as follows: copra, 34 per cent; desiccated coconut, 35 per cent; coconut oil, 96 per cent; and copra meal or cake, 63 per cent. The volume of exports of copper concentrates continued their upward trend, increasing 40 per cent over the two-year period. Bananas also became one of the ten leading exports, expanding in volume nearly 900 per cent. Sugar exports also performed well, rising 37 per cent in the period. Exports of logs and lumber, pineapples, and plywood did not change significantly. Another favorable development on the export side was the 26 per cent increase in the value of manufactured goods other than the processing of such products as sugar and coconuts. However, these exports still amounted to less than 0.7 per cent of all commodity exports.

NOTES

1. Central Bank of the Philippines, *Annual Report,* 1966, p. 1.

2. The new categories introduced into the Central Bank's commodity classification system at this time were defined as follows: unclassified producer (consumer) goods were goods produced in sufficient quantity to meet local demand and of acceptable quality and offered at competitive prices; semiunclassified producer (consumer) goods were goods that were produced locally but which did not fully satisfy the criteria for unclassified goods as to quantity, quality, or price. All goods not otherwise classified in the other categories were included in these two categories.

3. Sixto K. Roxas, "Exchange Rate Experience and Policy in the Philippines Since World War II," in H. Grubel and T. Morgan, eds., *Exchange Rate Policy in Southeast Asia* (Lexington, Mass.: Heath, 1973), p. 58.

4. Specifically, the following export activities were excluded from these credit ceilings:

a. The production of logs and lumber; sugar, copra, copra meal or cake; copper concentrates; coconut oil and desiccated coconut; abaca; plywood and veneer; canned pineapple; and other agricultural, forestry, marine, and base metal products;

b. The processing or manufacture of finished products for exportation, with an export potential as evidenced by export records or contracts and with an indigenous raw materials content of at least 70 per cent;

c. The processing or manufacture of finished products in which domestic value added is less than 50 per cent, but of which at least 50 per cent of total output is destined for export.

5. Later in the year, imports of machinery and spare parts for use by local wearing apparel and embroidery firms were added to the list of industries exempted from this requirement and also from the requirement that all imports be financed by letters of credit.

6. Imports of capital goods valued at over $20,000 were permitted after July 1969 only on a deferred payment basis (20 per cent down and payment terms of at least three years), and in November, prior approval of the Central Bank was required for imports of any single unit of machinery or equipment valued at over $50,000.

7. Only $500 per year could be obtained per adult resident of the Philippines for travel to North and South America, Europe, Japan, Australia, New Zealand, Africa, and the Middle East, and a $200 limit was set for travel to Hong Kong, Taipei, Okinawa, Guam, and other neighboring countries. In addition, formal regulations covering securities transactions involving foreign exchange were established.

8. An analysis by the BOI staff of selected income statements of proposed firms with respect to the extent of the aid provided by the act gives the following percentages for the ratio of the increase in profits due to tax assistance to the firm's total costs:

mechanical grain driers, 3; globe and gate valves, 3; hand pump manufacturing, 0.6; malleable iron fittings, 5; roller bearing units, 3; files, 7; and small gasoline engines, 7.

9. If one assumes all the revenue of the firms in the BOI sample was export revenue, the combined effect of the Investment Incentives and Export Incentives Acts gives the following percentage ratios for the increase in profits to the firm's total costs: mechanical grain driers, 8; globe and gate valves, 9; hand pump manufacturing, 2; malleable iron pipe fittings, 8; roller bearing units, 6; files, 7 (unchanged since these contain no raw materials); and small gasoline engines, 8.

10. Speech by President Marcos to Rotary Club of Manila, January 8, 1970, as reported in *Central Bank News Digest,* February 10, 1970, p. 6.

11. G. V. Soliven, "Management of External Debt," reported in *Central Bank News Digest,* July 13, 1971, p. 3.

12. G. S. Licaros, Speech before Rotary Club, February 26, 1970, as reported in *Central Bank News Digest,* March 10, 1970, p. 2.

13. The requirements that imports of capital goods with a unit value of over $20,000 be made only on a deferred payment basis and that importations of single units of machinery or equipment valued at over $50,000 could be made only with prior Central Bank approval also were continued.

14. In September, the requirement that monthly imports exceeding $50,000 receive prior Central Bank approval was also lifted for these firms. At the same time, imports of nonagricultural machinery and equipment in excess of $50,000 monthly were also permitted for firms not qualifying as export-oriented or registered with the BOI, provided the capital goods did not add to capacity in industries listed as overcrowded.

15. Concurrent with the freeing of the peso, the rediscount ceiling for domestic commercial banks was reduced from 125 per cent of paid-up capital plus 90 per cent of other net worth items as of June 20, 1967, to 100 per cent of paid-up capital as of December 31, 1969. That this change represented a reduction in rediscount ceilings was reported by Governor G. Licaros, "Impact of the Stabilization Program on the Development of the Philippine Economy" (Speech reported in *Central Bank News Digest,* November 3, 1970), p. 3.

16. In this period the Central Bank's external debt decreased $48 million, the national government's rose $34 million, and the volume of external credits extended to government corporations rose $48 million.

Chapter 5

Measures of Protection in the Philippines, 1950–71

As has been repeatedly brought out in the last three chapters, the Philippine government employed a wide variety of trade and payments measures as well as fiscal and monetary policies to attract resources to the manufacturing sector and to assist agriculture. These included such devices as exchange controls, protective tariffs, differential sales and compensating taxes, and exemptions from the payment of both domestic taxes and taxes imposed on imported inputs. Although the over-all picture of special incentives provided to the industrial sector is obvious, it is difficult to gain a clear view of the magnitude and relative differences among sectors in these incentives merely from an enumeration of the various policies. The purpose of the present chapter, consequently, is to analyze quantitatively the combined incentive effects of the different policies in terms of various pertinent measures, including effective exchange rates, implicit rates of protection, and effective protective rates.[1]

EFFECTIVE EXCHANGE RATES

One very useful measure of intersectoral differences in the incentives provided by an industrialization program is the effective exchange rate (EER) for various types of transactions, i.e., the number of units of local currency actually paid or received per dollar of a given international transaction. In addition to taking account of the different exchange rates applicable to various types of transactions, the EERs calculated here include the differential impact on these transactions of tariffs, discriminatory sales or compensating taxes,

84

special foreign-exchange taxes, exemptions from various domestic taxes, subsidized borrowing rates, and margin-deposit requirements on imports. What the concept of EERs does not include, however, is any estimate of protective effects over and above these measures that are caused by quantitative restrictions on the volume of foreign exchange available for a particular import.[2] But, if both c.i.f. and domestic prices are available, the ratio of the domestic price (net of normal distribution costs) of an imported commodity minus its c.i.f. import price (in local currency) to the c.i.f. import price, i.e., the implicit rate of protection, can be used to indicate the impact of either quantitative restrictions or explicitly protective measures. This section contains information on EERs; the next section contains an analysis of the pattern of implicit protection among exchange-control categories.

Tables 5-1, 5-2, and 5-3 contain sets of EERs between 1949 and 1971 for various commodity groups classified according to their degree of essentiality as determined by the exchange-control authorities (the Central Bank).[3] Table 5-2 contains price-level-deflated effective exchange rate (PLD-EERs), which are obtained by dividing the EERs in Table 5-1 by the Philippine wholesale price index. The exchange rates adjusted for purchasing power parity (PPP-EERs), shown in Table 5-3 are calculated, except for exports, by multiplying the EERs in Table 5-1 by the ratio of the U.S. wholesale price index to the Philippine wholesale price index. The export figures are estimated by multiplying the export EERs in Table 5-1 by the ratio of the index of unit values (in dollars) for Philippine exports to the Philippine wholesale price index.

Only from 1960 to November 1965 and again from February to May 1970 were there differences in the nominal exchange rates applicable to different categories of commodities. These differences are summarized in the appendix to this chapter, together with the unified rates that applied in the other years. Also specified in the appendix are the tariffs and other taxes or subsidies employed in calculating the effective exchange rates shown in Table 5-1.

There is considerable variation in the number of commodities included in each of the exchange-control groups listed in the tables, and it must be emphasized that the figures are presented as being typical of the commodity categories rather than as actual averages for the groups. The tariffs and other taxes used in calculating EERs for nonessential consumer goods are unweighted averages for Valdepeñas's 32-commodity sample of such goods.[4] Between 1949 and 1961 the essential producer goods category is represented by an unweighted average of Valdepeñas's sample of 53 goods.[5] From 1962 on, however, the degree of protection on mechanical and electrical equipment is used to represent the category.[6] Tax or subsidy rates for some of the other categories are also based only on a few representative commodities. The tariff and other taxes applicable to thermos bottles are used to represent the semi-

TABLE 5-1

Effective Exchange Rates, 1949–71

(pesos per U.S. dollar)

Category	1949	1950	1951	1952	1953	1954	1955	1956	1957	1958	1959	1960
Imports												
Consumer goods												
Nonessential	2.05	2.05	3.39	3.39	3.39	3.34	3.68	3.86	4.12	4.17	5.06	6.97
Semiessential	2.05	2.05	2.42	2.42	2.42	2.37	2.38	2.60	2.40	2.67	2.83	4.38
Essential	2.00	2.00	2.03	2.03	2.03	2.04	2.04	2.11	2.10	2.10	2.16	2.24
Producer goods												
Nonessential	2.05	2.05	2.42	2.42	2.42	2.36	2.38	2.51	2.50	2.52	2.67	4.25
Semiessential	2.00	2.00	2.37	2.37	2.37	2.37	2.37	2.45	2.48	2.50	3.07	3.10
Essential	2.00	2.00	2.37	2.37	2.37	2.37	2.38	2.48	2.48	2.51	3.09	3.12
For "new and necessary" industries	2.00	2.00	2.00	2.00	2.00	2.00	2.00	2.00	2.00	2.03	2.03	2.08
Exports												
Traditional	2.00	2.00	2.00	2.00	2.00	2.00	2.00	2.00	2.00	2.00	2.00	2.22
New	2.24	2.24	2.24	2.24	2.32	2.32	2.32	2.32	2.32	2.32	2.30	2.51

(*continued*)

TABLE 5-1 (*concluded*)

Category	1961	1962	1963	1964	1965	1966	1967	1968	1969	1970	1971
Imports											
Consumer goods											
Nonessential	7.02	10.04	11.24	11.10	11.95	11.69	11.77	11.91	11.94	17.67	19.26
Semiessential	4.46	4.95	5.54	5.47	5.65	5.49	5.53	5.61	5.62	8.33	9.11
Essential	3.15	3.74	4.24	4.24	4.29	4.29	4.29	4.29	4.29	6.48	7.04
Producer goods											
Nonessential	4.28	6.55	7.45	7.38	7.90	7.75	7.79	7.84	7.87	11.74	12.81
Semiessential	4.04	4.06	4.53	4.46	4.45	4.34	4.38	4.43	4.44	6.60	7.23
Essential	4.06	4.42	4.89	4.86	4.99	4.92	4.93	4.97	4.95	7.43	7.62
For "new and necessary" industries	2.92	3.44	3.90	3.90	3.90	3.90	3.90	3.90	3.90	5.89	6.40
Exports											
Traditional	2.68	3.15	3.52	3.52	3.90	3.90	3.90	3.90	3.90	5.15	5.76
New	2.95	3.37	3.72	3.72	4.13	4.13	4.17	4.17	4.17	6.54	7.26

SOURCE: See text.

TABLE 5-2

Effective Exchange Rates Deflated by the Wholesale Price Index, 1949–71

(pesos per U.S. dollar; 1955 = 100 for the wholesale price index)

Category	1949	1950	1951	1952	1953	1954	1955	1956	1957	1958	1959	1960
Imports												
Consumer goods												
Nonessential	1.87	1.92	2.84	3.09	3.12	3.26	3.68	3.74	3.83	3.75	4.49	5.94
Semiessential	1.87	1.92	2.02	2.21	2.23	2.31	2.38	2.52	2.24	2.40	2.51	3.73
Essential	1.82	1.88	1.70	1.86	1.87	1.99	2.04	2.05	1.95	1.89	1.92	1.98
Producer goods												
Nonessential	1.87	1.92	2.02	2.21	2.23	2.30	2.38	2.43	2.32	2.27	2.37	3.62
Semiessential	1.82	1.88	1.99	2.18	2.20	2.32	2.37	2.38	2.30	2.25	2.72	2.64
Essential	1.82	1.88	1.99	2.18	2.20	2.32	2.38	2.41	2.30	2.26	2.74	2.66
For "new and necessary" industries	1.81	1.87	1.67	1.82	1.84	1.95	2.00	1.93	1.85	1.83	1.80	1.77
Exports												
Traditional	1.82	1.88	1.67	1.83	1.85	1.95	2.00	1.94	1.86	1.80	1.77	1.89
New	2.04	2.10	1.87	2.05	2.10	2.26	2.32	2.25	2.16	2.09	2.04	2.14

(*continued*)

TABLE 5-2 (concluded)

Category	1961	1962	1963	1964	1965	1966	1967	1968	1969	1970	1971
Imports											
Consumer goods											
Nonessential	5.70	7.76	7.92	7.47	7.87	7.38	7.09	6.98	6.95	8.60	8.10
Semiessential	3.62	3.82	3.90	3.68	3.72	3.46	3.33	3.29	3.27	4.06	3.83
Essential	2.56	2.89	2.99	2.85	2.82	2.71	2.58	2.51	2.49	3.16	2.96
Producer goods											
Nonessential	3.47	5.06	5.25	4.97	5.20	4.89	4.69	4.59	4.58	5.72	5.39
Semiessential	3.28	3.14	3.19	3.00	2.93	2.74	2.64	2.59	2.58	3.21	3.04
Essential	3.30	3.42	3.44	3.27	3.28	3.10	2.97	2.91	2.88	3.62	3.21
For "new and necessary" industries	2.37	2.67	2.75	2.62	2.57	2.45	2.34	2.27	2.26	2.87	2.69
Exports											
Traditional	2.18	2.43	2.48	2.37	2.57	2.46	2.35	2.28	2.27	2.51	2.42
New	2.39	2.60	2.62	2.50	2.72	2.72	2.51	2.44	2.43	3.18	3.05

SOURCE: See text.

TABLE 5-3

Effective Exchange Rates Adjusted for Purchasing Power Parity, 1949–71

(pesos per U.S. dollar; 1955 = 100 for underlying price indices)

Category	1949	1950	1951	1952	1953	1954	1955	1956	1957	1958	1959	1960
Imports												
Consumer goods												
Nonessential	1.67	1.79	2.94	3.12	3.12	3.25	3.68	3.87	4.07	4.04	4.85	6.42
Semiessential	1.67	1.79	2.10	2.23	2.23	2.30	2.38	2.60	2.37	2.58	2.71	4.03
Essential	1.63	1.75	1.76	1.88	1.87	1.99	2.04	2.11	2.07	2.03	2.07	2.06
Producer goods												
Nonessential	1.67	1.79	2.10	2.23	2.23	2.29	2.38	2.51	2.47	2.44	2.56	3.91
Semiessential	1.63	1.75	2.06	2.20	2.19	2.30	2.37	2.46	2.45	2.42	2.94	2.85
Essential	1.63	1.75	2.06	2.20	2.19	2.30	2.38	2.49	2.45	2.43	2.96	2.87
For "new and necessary" industries	1.63	1.75	1.74	1.83	1.84	1.94	2.00	2.00	1.98	1.97	1.94	1.91
Exports												
Traditional	n.a.	2.57	2.46	2.00	2.47	2.18	2.00	1.96	1.93	1.89	2.15	2.34
New	n.a.	2.88	2.76	2.24	2.86	2.53	2.32	2.28	2.24	2.32	2.47	2.65

(*continued*)

TABLE 5-3 (concluded)

Category	1961	1962	1963	1964	1965	1966	1967	1968	1969	1970	1971
Imports											
Consumer goods											
Nonessential	6.13	8.37	8.52	8.05	8.65	8.39	8.07	8.15	8.43	10.81	10.51
Semiessential	3.53	4.13	4.20	3.97	4.09	3.93	3.79	3.84	3.97	5.10	4.97
Essential	2.75	3.12	3.21	3.08	3.11	3.08	2.94	2.93	3.02	3.96	3.84
Producer goods											
Nonessential	3.73	5.46	5.64	5.35	5.72	5.56	5.34	5.36	5.56	7.18	6.99
Semiessential	3.53	3.38	3.43	3.24	3.22	3.16	3.01	3.02	3.13	4.04	3.94
Essential	3.55	3.68	3.70	3.53	3.61	3.52	3.38	3.40	3.49	4.54	4.16
For "new and necessary" industries	2.55	2.87	2.96	2.83	2.83	2.78	2.66	2.65	2.74	3.61	3.49
Exports											
Traditional	2.61	3.10	3.66	3.62	4.00	3.90	3.97	4.09	3.98	5.57	5.62
New	2.88	3.32	3.86	3.82	4.24	4.13	4.24	4.37	4.26	7.08	7.08

n.a. = not available.
SOURCE: See text.

essential-consumer-goods group and the rates for canned milk and antibiotics, the essential-consumer-goods category.[7] Nonessential producer goods are represented by loudspeakers; and semiessential producer goods, by aqua ammonia.[8] Producer goods used by "new and necessary" industries cover those producer goods that were exempted from paying import taxes throughout the period.[9] Finally, new exports cover those manufacturers who received tax-exempt treatment and loans at below-market interest charges, and the traditional export group is represented by such agricultural exports as sugar, copra, and coconut oil.

The Structure of Effective Exchange Rates, 1949–71.

A consideration of the changes over the period in the differential incentives provided for the local production of nonessential consumer goods, essential consumer goods, producer goods used in "new and necessary" industries, and new exports not only brings out the types of measures included in the estimates of EERs in Table 5-1 but also indicates the basic nature of Philippine protectionist policies. Since there was a unified exchange rate in the Philippines until 1960, differences in EERs among various types of transactions up to that year are due only to differences in taxes or subsidies applicable to those transactions. In 1949 and 1950, American goods still entered the Philippines duty-free, and the sales or compensating tax was not yet discriminatory between imports and domestic production. The only barrier to importation was and 80 per cent margin-deposit requirement on luxury and nonessential items. On the basis of a 12 per cent interest rate and an average three-month holding period for the deposit, this is equivalent to an additional import cost of 2.4 per cent. The EER for nonessential goods was, therefore 1.024 × P2.00 = P2.05 per dollar. In Table 5-1 this rate is listed for nonessential consumer goods, while the official rate of P2.00 per dollar is given for essential consumer goods and producer goods used in "new and necessary" industries.

The EERs in Table 5-1 on new exports are to be interpreted as equal to the official rate plus the subsidy rate on annual sales for producers of these products. It is assumed that these firms could borrow from such government institutions as the Development Bank of the Philippines at 2 per cent below the free-market rate. From 1949 through 1962, assistance to firms producing new exports consisted of exemption from a varying proportion of internal taxes and duties on imports of capital goods, as well as easy financing terms (see the appendix to this chapter for more details). In 1949 and 1950 the combined tax and borrowing subsidy to producers of new exports was 12.2 per cent, a figure that yields an EER per dollar of P2.24 (= 1.122 × P2.00).

The pattern of a high degree of protection from import competition to domestic producers of nonessential goods and a low degree of protection to local producers of essential consumer goods and essential producer goods began to emerge by 1951. Tariffs were still not being imposed on U.S. imports because of the preferences granted American goods, but the base of the sales tax on luxury items was changed to grant protection to local producers equivalent to a 50 per cent duty. A slight degree of protection, 1.75 per cent, resulted from similar sales tax changes for essential consumer goods. In addition, the special 17 per cent excise tax on sales of foreign exchange was levied in 1951, but with essential consumer goods and capital goods for "new and necessary" industries being exempted from this tax. Thus, in addition to the protective effects of the 80 per cent margin-deposit requirement (0.024 × P2.00 = P0.05), the EER for imports of nonessential consumer goods exceeded the official figure of P2 per dollar both because of the discriminatory sales tax (0.5 × P2.00 = P1.00) and the 17 per cent special excise tax on foreign exchange sales (0.17 × P2.00 = P0.34). The combined impact of these taxes is an EER of P2.00 + P0.05 + P1.00 + P0.34 = P3.39 per U.S. dollar. The EER for imports of essential consumer goods in 1951 was 1.0175 × P2.00 = P2.03 per dollar. Since no import taxes were levied on producer goods for new industries, the EER for this group remained at P2.00 per dollar. Imports of a dollar's worth of nonessential consumer goods, therefore, cost Philippine importers nearly 70 per cent more than a dollar's worth of producer goods for new industries. Various tax exemptions and low-cost borrowing privileges extended to firms producing new exports again amounted to 12.2 per cent of sales and maintained an EER of P2.24 per dollar.

The protection provided local producers of nonessential goods continued to rise throughout the 1950s for several reasons. Most important were the gradual reduction in the degree of preferential treatment for U.S. goods and the substantial increase, in 1957, in tariffs on luxury goods. As these occurred, additional protection was provided by the discriminatory sales tax, which was based on the c.i.f.-plus-duty price of imports. The special 25 per cent margin fee on foreign exchange was also introduced in 1959. On the other hand, essential consumer goods were subject only to a rather modest tariff and a small discriminatory sales tax, while essential producer goods for "new and necessary" industries were not subject even to those taxes.[10]

During the early part of the decontrol period, 1960 and 1961, the increase in the cost of a dollar from 2 pesos to 3.0 pesos acted to raise the EER for nonessential consumer goods, whereas the gradual decline in the special import tax (the replacement for the tax on foreign exchange) and in the margin fee operated to reduce it. On balance, however, this rate rose from P5.06 per dollar in 1959 to P7.02 in 1961. In 1962, the decline in the margin fee on foreign-exchange sales, from 15 per cent to zero, was more than offset by the additional depreciation of the peso to P3.90 per dollar, the rise in the average statutory duty level for the sample of goods in this category from 51 per cent to 83 per cent, the increase in the proportion of Philippine tariffs applicable to American goods from 50 per cent to 75 per cent, and the introduction of a special time-deposit requirement for imports. As a result, the EER for nonessential consumer goods jumped to P10.04 per dollar. This rate increased somewhat further in 1965 when the share of Philippine duties applicable to U.S. goods rose from 75 per cent to 90 per cent, producing a stronger upward impact than the decline in the special import tax. Throughout the rest of the 1960s, variations in required margin deposits against imports were the only cause of changes in the EER for nonessential consumer goods, and did not significantly affect it. However, in 1970 the depreciation of the peso to an average of nearly P6 per dollar again brought about a substantial rise in the EER for nonessential consumer goods.

As is indicated in Table 5-1, until 1961, when the exchange rate for imports of essential consumer goods was increased above the traditional level of P2 per dollar, the EER for these goods rose only slightly, while the rate on producer goods for new industries remained unchanged. Fixing the exchange rate at P3.90 per dollar, in mid-1962, acted to raise the EERs for these two classes of imports significantly. Other forces influencing the level of EERs in that year were a reduction in the statutory duty rates on many essential consumer goods, the rise in the proportion of tariff rates that were applicable to imports from the United States (relevant only for essential consumer goods, since imports of producer goods for new industries were exempt from import duties), and the elimination of the margin fee on sales of foreign exchange (applicable only to producer goods for new industries, since essential consumer goods were exempted from this charge). The net impact of these factors was an increase in the EERs for essential consumer goods to P3.74 per dollar and for producer goods used in "new and necessary" industries to P3.44 per dollar. The EER for essential goods again rose in 1963, but then changed little until 1970. The rate for "new and necessary" industries remained at P3.90 per dollar from 1962 to 1969.

The EER that applied to new exports increased in 1960 due to a rise in the official exchange rate for new exports to P2.30 per dollar. This increase, coupled with tax and interest subsidies, which declined somewhat from 1959, brought about an increase in the effective rate for this category from P2.30 to P2.51 per dollar between 1959 and 1960. Through the mid-1960s, the main factors affecting this rate were increases in the exchange rate applicable to export transactions, first to P3.5 per dollar in 1962 and then to P3.90 per dollar in 1965. The Investment Incentives Act of 1967 provided a slight increase in the EER, but the major increase after 1965 occurred in 1970 with the peso depreciation and the increase in export subsidies associated with the Export Incentives Act of 1970.

As is clearly brought out in Table 5-1, the Philippine government employed exchange-rate, fiscal, and monetary policies to increase sharply the peso costs of importing so-called nonessential consumer and producer goods. In the late 1940s and early 1950s nonessential consumer goods tended to consist of items consumed only by the higher income groups, while nonessential producer goods tended to comprise the raw materials and capital goods needed to produce these nonessential consumer goods. As the 1950s progressed, however, these categories were used more and more to protect from import competition those commodities that government officials decided could be produced domestically in acceptable quality and without incurring unreasonably high costs. As noted in Chapter 2, one exchange-control category, namely, unclassified items, consisted of commodities which in the opinion of government officials were in adequate local supply and whose importation was, therefore, virtually banned. Many items in the nonessential groups were given even greater protection by shifting them into this unclassified group.

TABLE 5-4

**Relationships Among Effective Exchange Rates for
Various Exchange-Control Categories, 1950–70**

Ratios of Categories[a]	1950	1955	1960	1965	1970
NEC to EC	1.02	1.80	3.12	2.78	2.72
SEC to EC	1.00	1.55	1.87	1.32	1.28
NEC to TX	1.02	1.84	3.14	3.06	3.43
SEC to TX	1.02	1.19	1.93	1.45	1.62
NEC to NX	0.92	1.59	2.78	2.80	2.70
EC to NX	0.89	0.88	0.89	1.04	0.99

SOURCE: Table 5-1, above.

a. The abbreviations stand for the following exchange-control categories: NEC, nonessential consumer goods; EC, essential consumer goods; SEC, semiessential consumer goods; TX, traditional exports; and NX, new exports.

As is clearly expressed by the data in Table 5-4, between 1950 and 1960 the EERs among exchange-control categories changed in such a manner that there was a strong incentive to shift resources from the production of essential items and export products to the production of nonessential and semiessential goods.[11] The most important point to be made about the decontrol efforts in the early 1960s and developments during the rest of the 1960s is that they did not restore EERs for the various groups of imports to those observed prior to the exchange-control period. However, the incentives favoring the production of nonessential and semiessential consumer goods relative to essential consumer goods and exports were generally weaker in 1970 than in 1960.

Real Changes in Effective Exchange Rates, 1949–71.

The price-level-deflated effective exchange rates (PLD-EERs) in Table 5-2 as well as the purchasing-power-parity-adjusted effective exchange rates (PPP-EERs) in Table 5-3 also bring out the protective aspects of Philippine trade policy as well as the adverse effects of this policy on exporters. Except for essential consumer goods and essential producer goods used in "new and necessary" industries, the real peso cost of a dollar's worth of imports, i.e., the PLD-EER, increased substantially during the 1950s. For the sample of nonessential consumer goods, the rise between 1949 and 1959 was 140 per cent,[12] while for essential consumer goods, the increase was only 5 per cent. On the other hand, the domestic purchasing power of a dollar's worth of exports actually decreased 3 per cent between these years. Of course, these relationships ignore changes in world market prices. Using changes in U.S. wholesale prices to indicate the international purchasing power of a dollar, the PPP-EER (i.e., the EER multiplied by the ratio of U.S. wholesale prices to Philippine wholesale prices) for imports of nonessential and essential consumer goods increased by 190 per cent and 27 per cent, respectively, between 1949 and 1959. As previously noted, in order to indicate changes in the quantity of Philippine exports needed to earn a dollar, the unit value (in dollars) export index of the Philippines is used rather than the U.S. wholesale price index. The ratio of this price index to the Philippine wholesale price index multiplied by the effective exchange rate for traditional exports, i.e., the PPP-EER, decreased 16 per cent between 1950 and 1959 (24 per cent between 1950 and 1956), indicating that the domestic purchasing power of exporters was considerably poorer at the end of the decade than at the beginning.

The elimination of exchange controls reversed this downward trend in the purchasing-power position of exporters. For example, the PPP-EER for traditional exports increased 44 per cent between 1959 and 1962. The impact of the exchange-rate liberalization on producers of import substitutes cannot be completely determined from Tables 5-1, 5-2, and 5-3 because of the existence of quantitative import controls in 1959. However, wholesale prices of such items as nonessential and unclassified consumer goods (see Table 5-6, below) increased less than wholesale prices in general between 1959 and 1962, whereas the opposite is true of essential producer goods. Moreover, the price increase in producer goods shown in Table 5-6 understates the actual cost increase of these goods for producers who imported them directly, since the 1959 wholesale price of producer goods shown in the table includes the windfall gains associated with quantitative controls. Thus, the liberalization measures shifted production incentives in favor of exporters and against producers of manufactured consumer goods in the nonessential and unclassified categories.

One important consequence of these shifts in incentives (which was discussed in Chapter 3) was the relative movement of resources into export production and out of food production. The result was a substantial increase in food prices and therefore a significant rise in the wholesale price index for all items, especially between 1962 and 1965. Since nominal EERs increased for all categories of import commodities as well as for exports between 1962 and 1965, and U.S. wholesale prices rose only moderately, this significant rise in Philippine wholesale prices caused the PPP-EER for several import groups actually to decline between these years.

Between 1965 and 1969 the PPP-EERs for all import categories declined, while those for exports did not change. The development efforts of the Marcos administration as well as the election-related program of monetary and fiscal ease of 1969 caused Philippine wholesale prices to rise somewhat relative to U.S. wholesale prices and thus brought about a decline in the real cost of imports. The ratio of the dollar price of Philippine exports to U.S. wholesale prices did not change significantly. However, the floating of the peso in early 1970 and its consequent depreciation sharply increased the PDL-EER and PPP-EER for both imports and exports.

The main point that emerges from an overview of the more than twenty-year period covered in Table 5-3 is the very significant increase in the real costs of importing commodities, especially nonessential goods. By 1971, the PPP-EER for nonessential consumer goods was more than six times as high as in 1949, while the PPP-EER for nonessential producer goods was over four times as high in 1971 as in 1949. On the other hand, the domestic purchasing power of traditional exports was only 2.2 times as high in 1971 as in 1950. The widening of the gap between the real costs of importing nonessentials and the domestic purchasing power of traditional exports occurred during the period of exchange controls in the 1950s. For example, the ratio of the PPP-EER for nonessential consumer goods to the PPP-EER for traditional exports rose from 0.7 in 1950 to 2.3 in 1959. Even the disparity in 1959 underestimates the ratio of the consumer costs of importing to the real rewards of exporters, since importers were able to add on a scarcity windfall gain to their import costs due to the existence of exchange controls. The 1960 level of 2.7 for this ratio more accurately reflects the true differential, since the exchange rate on nonessentials was raised in that year to eliminate much of the windfall gain accruing to importers. During the rest of the 1960s and into the early 1970s, the gap between real importing costs and real export rewards narrowed. The ratio of the PPP-EERs for nonessential consumer goods to traditional exports was only 2.2 in 1965 and 1.9 in 1971. However, the ratio is still much higher than it had been during the immediate postwar period, indicating the continued existence of a pattern of incentives strongly favoring import-substituting investments in nonessential lines relative to the expansion of traditional (and even new) exports.

IMPLICIT RATES OF PROTECTION

Although EERs after 1962 provide a good indication of the relative incentives made available to different types of manufacturing activity, as already noted, such rates prior to that time underestimate the levels of protection because of the existence of exchange controls. What is needed for estimating incentive effects of import controls when quantitative restrictions are binding is a comparison of domestic and import prices. Unfortunately, in the case of the Philippines, unit-value import prices for individual commodities computed from the most detailed import data available from the Central Bank vary so much over time as to cast serious doubt on the validity of the quantity figures for particular items. However, adequate c.i.f. and domestic comparisons for certain commodities do exist for the years 1950 and 1951 because special studies of this relationship were made by the government in connection with price control efforts of that time. The implicit protective rates obtained from this data can then be tied in with time-series information on price changes to indicate changes in the pattern of implicit tariffs over time.

Table 5-5 contains price comparisons for a selected list of items as of December 1951. As is indicated in the table, the range of implicit protection was very wide, going from nearly 400 per cent to almost 700 per cent on such luxury items as oranges, cigarettes, and salt to quite moderate levels on evaporated and condensed milk. On the other hand, as can be seen from Table 5-1, the protection afforded a given import bundle of nonessential consumer goods by explicit fiscal and monetary measures in 1951 was only 70 per cent, i.e. [(3.39/2.00) − 1.00] × 100.[13] The comparable figure for essential consumer goods was 2 per cent.

Domestic price behavior of the imported commodities included in the wholesale price index is shown in Table 5-6 on the basis of essentiality categories. As is indicated in the table, after the Korean War boom the government permitted prices of both essential consumer goods and essential producer goods to drop from their 1951 peak levels. But the high levels of the less essential consumer and producer goods were left unchanged. In a sense the government was able to use the temporarily high prices of the early 1950s as an umbrella under which to carry out its discrimination among commodity groups without facing consumer complaints that prices were actually being increased.

TABLE 5-5

Implicit Protection on Selected Commodities, December 1951

	Retail Price	C.I.F. Import Price	Excess of Adj. Retail Price[a] Over C.I.F. Price
Essential consumer goods			
Corned beef (12 oz.)	P0.90	P0.39	111%
Salmon (lb.)	1.13	0.47	120
Sardines (14 oz.)	0.53	0.31	51
Milk, evaporated (can)	0.39	0.29	14
Milk, condensed (can)	0.65	0.47	18
Flour, wheat (kilo)	0.59	0.26	107
Average[b]			70
Nonessential consumer goods			
Cocoa, Peter's (half-lb.)	0.96	0.40	120
Oranges (doz.)	1.93	0.38	388
Coffee, roasted (lb.)	4.00	1.01	276
Cotton cloth, dyed (yd.)	1.65	0.54	186
Cotton cloth, printed (yd.)	1.50	0.62	122
Cigarettes (pkg.)	0.85	0.16	411
Apples (doz.)	1.40	0.46	184
Salt, refined (lb.)	0.65	0.08	694
Average[b]			297
Essential producer goods			
Galvanized iron, corrugated (sheet)	10.55	6.37	46
Kerosene (can)	4.13	0.76	423
Diesel fuel oil (liter)	0.19	0.08	118
Gasoline (liter)	0.24	0.05	360
Average[b]			236
Nonessential producer goods			
Cocoa seeds (ganta[c])	6.00	2.80	93
Starch (kilo)	0.75	0.33	107
Average[b]			100
Unclassified items			
Onions (kilo)	0.55	0.20	155
Garlic (kilo)	1.61	0.41	273
Average[b]			214

SOURCE: Central Bank of the Philippines, *Annual Report*, 1951, p. 18.

a. In calculating implicit rates, 20 per cent of the c.i.f. import price is subtracted from the retail price, since on most items, the price control authorities allowed this margin between retail and import prices.

b. Unweighted averages.

c. This measure, which is peculiar to the Philippines, equals 3 liters.

TABLE 5-6

Wholesale Price Indices[a] for Imported Commodities
Classified by Degree of Essentiality, 1951–70
(1949 = 100)

	1951	1955	1959	1962	1966	1969	1970[b]
Essential consumer goods (EC)	128	107	125	183	208	214	322
Nonessential consumer goods (NEC)	155	163	281	308	325	348	488
Unclassified consumer goods (UC)	134	127	188	212	211	234	312
Essential producer goods (EP)	160	136	156	188	197	205	257
Semiessential producer goods (SEP)	130	132	201	222	241	252	328
Unclassified producer goods (UP)	173	106	142	158	165	160	183

SOURCE: Central Bank of the Philippines.

a. The 1970 essentiality classification of the Central Bank was used to divide the items included in the wholesale price index into the various groups. The number of items used to compute the simple means in each group are as follows: EC—11 for 1951 and 1955 and 16 thereafter; NEC—26 items for 1951 and 1955 and 39 items thereafter; UC—6 items for 1951 and 1955 and 17 items thereafter; EP—16 items for the entire period; SEP—4 items for 1951 and 1955 and 15 items thereafter; UP—13 items for 1951 and 1955 and 26 items thereafter. Semiessential goods and semiunclassified producer goods are not included because the sample size for these items was too small.

b. As of September.

After 1955, however, all prices again rose with the result that by 1959 prices of essential goods were again at their 1951 levels. Prices of nonessential consumer and producer goods continued to rise to new highs, with the degree of discrimination between nonessential and essential consumer goods widening from 56 in 1955 to 156 in 1959. Moreover, since the Central Bank's index of c.i.f. import unit values for total imports actually declined about 2 per cent between 1951 and 1959, it seems that the increases in wholesale prices of imported goods in the Philippines between 1951 and 1959 reflect changes in the degree of implicit protection rather than increases in c.i.f. costs.[14]

It is difficult to estimate average levels of implicit protection by exchange-control groups because of the wide variations in the degree of protection among commodities and the small size of the sample in Table 5-5. However, if this sample is representative, implicit rates of 200 per cent or more in 1951 were not unusual for nonessential consumer goods. Since, as is indicated in Table 5-6, prices of this group of items rose about 80 per cent between 1951 and 1959, levels of implicit protection of 400 per cent or more apparently existed at this time for some items.[15] The protection from explicit fiscal measures on this category of goods was 149 per cent, and this implies that windfall gains of over 200 per cent were being made on these commodities.

A more comprehensive estimate of the degree of protection of nonessential consumer goods in 1959 can be made by working backward from the behavior of import prices and domestic wholesale prices for this category between 1959 and 1962, when import controls were completely dismantled. The remarkable thing is that, whereas the peso cost, inclusive of all taxes, of a dollar's worth of nonessential consumer goods rose by 98 per cent over this period (Table 5-1) primarily as a result of the devaluation of the peso, the wholesale price index for these goods rose by only about 10 per cent (Table 5-6). This disparity is indicative of the large windfall gains which had been accruing to importers and traders in 1959 and which were eliminated with the freeing of imports from controls. In contrast to the explicit protection of 149 per cent, i.e. $[(5.06/2.03) - 1.00] \times 100$, provided by fiscal and monetary measures for nonessential consumer goods in 1959 (Table 5-1), the implicit protective rate at that time can be calculated at about 361 per cent.[16] Similar calculations for essential consumer goods and for essential producer goods give implicit rates of protection in 1959 of 30 and 88 per cent, respectively.

A third method of estimating levels of implicit protection in the 1950s is to compare wholesale prices of comparable items in the Philippines and the United States. The results for a selected list of goods for which this comparison was possible are presented in Table 5-7. If it is assumed that costs of shipping from U.S. wholesalers to Philippine wholesalers equals 25 per cent of the U.S. price, the protection on evaporated milk in 1959 amounts to 14 per cent, a figure comparable to that in Table 5-5.[17] For such nonessential consumer goods as canned cherries, canned asparagus, canned peaches, and coffee, the implicit protective rates on the basis of the same kind of calculation were 426, 374, 159, and 197 per cent, respectively, in 1959. On the other hand, in the essential-producer-goods group, the 1959 protective rate on standard American newsprint was only 16 per cent; for sodium bichromate, 31 per cent; and for blasting caps, 75 per cent.

It is clear from these three estimates that exchange controls added greatly to the degree of protection provided by explicit fiscal and monetary measures. In 1959, for example, implicit protective rates of 400 per cent were not uncommon for nonessential consumer goods, whereas the average explicit degree of protection in 1959 for this category was around 150 per cent. For the essential-consumer-goods group, average implicit and explicit protective rates in the same year were roughly 30 and 5 per cent, respectively.

TABLE 5-7

**Selected U.S. Wholesale Prices and Wholesale Prices of Comparable
Imported Goods in the Philippines, 1949–65**

(U.S. dollars[a])

Description[b]	1949	1956	1959	1962	1965
Evaporated milk (EC), case of 48, 14½ oz. tins					
Philippines	7.20	7.96	9.28	7.47	8.08
United States	—	6.00	6.52	6.07	6.31
Canned cherries (NEC), doz. cans					
Philippines	—	—	12.00	7.14	7.66
United States	—	—	1.82	1.81	1.86
Canned peaches (NEC), doz. cans					
Philippines	—	—	8.75	4.97	5.26
United States	—	—	2.70	2.42	3.07
Canned asparagus (NEC), doz. cans					
Philippines	—	10.62	13.88	8.10	8.74
United States	—	2.41	2.34	2.50	2.62
Coffee (NEC), 1 lb. tin					
Philippines	—	2.34	2.64	1.41	1.44
United States	—	1.00	0.71	0.64	0.80
Cocoa beans (NEP), lb.					
Philippines	0.44	0.75	1.08	0.53	0.55
United States	0.21	0.27	0.31	0.21	0.21
Denim (UP), yd.					
Philippines	0.44	0.52	0.60	0.40	0.51
United States	0.31	0.36	0.37	0.38	0.35
Standard American newsprint (EP), ton					
Philippines	—	171.00	194.00	136.00	168.00
United States	100.00	130.00	134.00	134.00	132.00
Sodium bichromate (EP), lb.					
Philippines	—	0.20	0.21	0.14	0.18
United States	0.10	0.13	0.13	0.13	0.13
Potash muriate, basis 58–60% K_2O (EP), ton					
Philippines	—	93.00	106.00	64.00	86.00
United States	29.00	23.00	20.00	23.00	24.00
Blasting caps, ordinary (EP), 1,000					
Philippines	—	32.00	48.00	45.00	30.00
United States	—	20.00	22.00	23.00	24.00

SOURCE: Philippine data from Central Bank of the Philippines; U.S. data from U.S. Department of Commerce, Bureau of Labor Statistics.

a. The conversion rate was 2 pesos to the dollar for 1946–59 and 3.90 pesos to the dollar for 1962 and 1965.

b. EC = essential consumer goods; NEC = nonessential consumer goods; EP = essential producer goods; NEP = nonessential producer goods; UP = unclassified producer goods.

The relative protection afforded the different commodity categories remained essentially the same between 1962 and 1969, since the ratio of non-essential-consumer-goods prices to essential-consumer-goods prices and that of essential-producer-goods prices to essential-consumer-goods prices in 1969 were 1.63 and 0.96, respectively, compared to 1.68 and 1.03 in 1962. Absolute levels of implicit protection also did not change appreciably, as wholesale prices of imported goods increased in roughly the same proportion as import unit values.

A comparison of the change in EERs and the change in wholesale prices of imported goods between 1969 and 1970 suggests that some windfall gains due to exchange controls may have existed in 1969, because wholesale prices rose less than the peso prices of foreign commodities. This seems to hold particularly in the essential-producer-goods category for which, even assuming no rise in c.i.f. prices, the peso cost of imports increased 50 per cent, whereas the price index rose only 25 per cent. However, an examination of the individual prices in this index reveals that many are reported as unchanged between 1969 and September 1970 (and some even since 1966). One suspects that for many of these specialized capital goods, many wholesalers did not sell any of these items between the time the exchange rate was depreciated, in February 1970, and September 1970 and thus reported the price as unchanged from its 1969 level. Simply removing items for which there was no price change at all between 1969 and 1970 raises the price index in 1970 from 257 to 298 —a 45 per cent increase over the 1969 level. For other items, there probably were sales by some wholesalers, but the price index for the item is still biased downward because of the absence of sales by others.

EFFECTIVE PROTECTION

Some of the effective protective rates (EPRs) for the Philippines calculated by John Power are shown in Tables 5-8 and 5-9.[18] Power's estimates include the effects of the discriminatory sales or compensating tax[19] in addition to import duties, but not the effects of the margin fee on foreign exchange, the special import tax, or the margin requirements for letters of credit—measures that also provided protection against imports in 1965.

Power points out that the negative effective rates for canned meat and dairy products (Table 5-8) were obtained because of duty-free imports of these items made in 1965 by the National Marketing Corporation, a government organization whose function was to help maintain adequate supplies of essential consumer goods at low prices. He is somewhat skeptical about the accuracy of the negative rates for such manufactured items as stationery but suggests that production inefficiencies may be so extensive in some industries as to result in negative effective rates at world market prices.

TABLE 5-8

Nominal and Effective Rates of Protection in Import-competing Manufacturing Industries in the Philippines, 1965

ISIC Code	Industry	Nominal Protection	Effective Protection
2014	Canned meat	5%	−70%
2024	Dairy products	1	−26
3832	Vehicle engines, parts, bodies	18	4
3621	Agricultural tractors	14	5
3622	Farm machinery, except tractors	16	5
3392	Lime	12	7
3632	Metal-forming machinery	12	8
3412	Iron and steel foundry products	10	7
3196	Agricultural chemicals	15	13
3111	Inorganic acids, alkali, chlorine	18	10
2056	Flour mill products	15	12
3651	Industrial pumps and compressors	16	14
3192	Pharmaceutical preparations	25	22
3319	Structural clay products	19	21
3113	Compressed and liquified gases	24	25
3092	Processed rubber	27	23
3646	Woodworking machinery	15	27
3199	Inks and dyes	30	34
3211	Petroleum refinery products	13	42
3511	Packers' cans	25	49
3021	Tires and inner tubes	51	52
3591	Metal barrels, drums, etc.	40	59
3641	Rice-milling machinery	41	65
2712	Paper and paperboard products	31	59
3831	Trucks and buses	29	75
3321	Glass containers	45	81
3322	Flat glass and mirrors	44	77
3198	Polishing preparations	51	91
3411	Steel mill products	29	88
3731	Batteries	50	92
3734	Electric wires and wiring devices	20	103
3114	Fertilizers	16	72
3551	Wire nails, brads, and spikes	29	107
3992	Fabricated plastic products	74	156
3532	Architectural metal work	60	151

(*continued*)

TABLE 5-8 (concluded)

ISIC Code	Industry	Nominal Protection	Effective Protection
3923	Eyeglasses and spectacles	98	165
3312	Clay tiles	102	243
3749	Sewing machines, household	78	318
3531	Structural iron and steel	81	335
3115	Plastic and resin materials	69	485
3732	Electric lamps	125	2,320
2641	Metal furniture	104	784
2721	Stationery	71	−2,600
3742	Industrial refrigerators and air conditioners	101	−447
2911	Leather	105	−461
2316	Jute mill products	110	−3,154
3722	Household radios, phonos, and TV	147	−604
3951	Jewelry	252	−323
	Average[a]	30	59

ISIC = International Standard Industrial Classification.
SOURCE: John H. Power, "The Structure of Protection in the Philippines," in Bela Balassa and associates, *The Structure of Protection in Developing Countries* (Baltimore: Johns Hopkins Press, 1971), p. 275.
a. Nominal rates are weighted by output and effective rates by "derived" free-trade value added.

The averages presented in Table 5-9 again confirm the disadvantageous position of export producers compared to domestic producers of import-competing manufactures. Power's 1965 estimates of EPRs are −19 per cent for the former group and 59 per cent for the latter. EPRs for various export industries that I calculated for 1965 are as follows: veneer and plywood, −14 per cent; lumber, −11; coconut and copra, −6; abaca and other fibers, −12; metallic mining, −16; and brewery and malt products, −9.[20]

A time series of EPRs by exchange-control categories, which is derived from tariff data and input coefficients collected by Valdepeñas[21] and also includes the effect of the other nontariff measures included in Table 5-1, is shown in Table 5-10. The manner in which these were derived is explained in detail in the appendix to this chapter. Briefly, the nominal protection (penalty or subsidy in the case of exports) is taken to be the percentage by which the EER in any year (Table 5-1) exceeds the EER for producer goods used by "new and necessary" industries in that year. Between 1949 and 1959, the

TABLE 5-9

**Average Rates of Protection[a]
in Philippine Manufacturing, 1965**

Industry Group	Nominal Protection	Effective Protection
Exports (excluding sugar)	−8%	−19%
Import-competing	30	59
Non-import-competing[b]	26	83
Sugar	35	183
All manufacturing	2	48
Except exports	28	71

SOURCE: Power, *Protection in the Philippines*, p. 278.

a. Nominal rates are weighted by output and effective rates by free-trade value added.

b. Non-import-competing industries are defined as those in which imports amount to less than 10 per cent of domestic production.

lowest EER rate was generally the official rate of P2.00 to the dollar.[22] Since the EER equals the peso purchase price of a dollar's worth of goods rather than the selling price of these goods—the latter figure exceeds the former if imports are quantitatively restricted—the nominal protection on output is an underestimate of the actual (implicit) level of protection during the period of import controls from 1949 to 1960.

The calculation of EPRs over time highlights the biases previously pointed out against the production of export commodities and essential goods and in favor of nonessential goods. In 1961, for example, the effective protection afforded domestic producers of nonessential consumer goods relative to producers of goods used by "new and necessary" industries was 230 per cent, whereas it was 39 per cent for firms specializing in essential producer goods. The unfavorable exchange rate for exporters together with the protection on the imported inputs they used caused the EPR for traditional exports to be significantly negative in that year. Moreover, the discrepancies in effective protective rates remain very large even after the decontrol effort and throughout the rest of the 1960s and early 1970s.

SMUGGLING AND OTHER MEANS OF EVASION

Open smuggling has long been a serious problem in the Philippines because of the physical features of the country, and no analysis of protection in the

TABLE 5-10

Effective Protective Rates, 1949–71

(per cent)

Category	1949	1950	1951	1952	1953	1954	1955	1956	1957	1958	1959	1960
Imports												
Consumer goods												
Nonessential	5	5	114	114	114	110	141	154	179	178	183	349
Semiessential	4	4	23	23	23	19	19	34	18	37	31	149
Essential	0	0	−7	−7	−7	−7	−8	−5	−6	−7	−18	−15
Producer goods												
Nonessential	5	5	24	24	24	17	19	28	26	25	5	173
Semiessential	0	0	19	19	19	19	21	22	24	24	51	52
Essential	0	0	19	19	19	19	20	23	24	24	52	50
For "new and necessary" industries	0	0	0	0	0	0	0	0	0	0	0	0
Exports												
Traditional	0	0	−15	−15	−15	−15	−16	−19	−19	−20	−43	−27
New (subsidy)	23	23	23	23	31	31	31	31	31	27	25	40

(continued)

TABLE 5-10 (concluded)

Category	1961	1962	1963	1964	1965	1966	1967	1968	1969	1970	1971
Imports											
Consumer goods											
Nonessential	230	337	332	326	365	354	357	363	365	354	362
Semiessential	61	54	53	50	56	50	52	54	55	51	57
Essential	−9	−2	0	0	0	1	1	1	1	2	5
Producer goods											
Nonessential	56	169	174	171	198	191	193	195	197	193	203
Semiessential	40	21	14	12	12	12	13	15	15	14	14
Essential	39	28	25	25	28	26	26	27	27	26	19
For "new and necessary" industries	0	0	0	0	0	0	0	0	0	0	0
Exports											
Traditional	−45	−37	−38	−38	−22	−20	−21	−22	−21	−43	−33
New (subsidy)	2	−4	−9	−9	12	12	13	13	13	21	26

SOURCE: See text.

country is complete without a discussion of this subject. American cigarettes, textiles, narcotics, and firearms appear to be the most important items smuggled into the country. In addition, a significant volume of copra and illegally cut logs is exported without passing through proper channels. The value of smuggled goods is, of course, very difficult to estimate. An estimate from the government's Anti-Smuggling Action Center places the annual value of smuggled cigarettes at about $37 million in the 1962–65 period and $9 million from 1966 to 1969. Although estimates of the influx of other smuggled goods are not available, the Anti-Smuggling Action Center does report the value of confiscations of these other goods. If the ratio of the total volume of cigarettes smuggled to the volume of cigarettes confiscated holds for these other goods, the total value of smuggled goods, including cigarettes, comes to about $19 million in both 1966 and 1969, or around 2 per cent of total imports.

More important than pure smuggling is so-called technical smuggling. This involves exporting or importing through regular ports but incorrectly valuing, declaring, or classifying the commodities. Underinvoicing of exports and overreporting of imports are well-recognized means of transferring funds abroad. Similarly, declaring imports to be in commodity categories with lower tariffs than those which actually apply and undervaluing imports are familiar methods for avoiding the payment of import taxes.

A comparison by George Hicks of export and import values as reported in Philippine statistics with exports and import values based on the statistics of the country's major trading partners is reported in Table 5-11. On this evidence, both exports and imports were generally undervalued during the 1950s and 1960s, presumably because of the importance of smuggling and the underinvoicing of both exports and imports. In the late 1950s it was estimated by Central Bank authorities that the country was losing at least 10 per cent of the annual dollar receipts from exports because of undervaluation and misdeclaration of the latter.[23] Clearly, the overvaluation of the peso during this period created a strong incentive for exporters to engage in these actions.[24] The degree of export undervaluation decreases after the 1962 devaluation (and is less than import undervaluation), consistent with the expected relationship between the exchange rate and the extent of underinvoicing of exports.

Undervaluation and misclassification of imports in categories where tariffs are high or exchange controls tight have also been serious problems for certain commodities. Textiles are the most frequently cited case. Ayal found, for example, that in 1965 the value of imports of textiles from the United States and from Japan as reported by the Central Bank was $6 and $9 million, respectively. At the same time, exports of textiles to the Philippines from the United States, as reported by the U.S. embassy, were $29 million and from

TABLE 5-11

**Official Philippine Exports and Imports as Percentages of Totals Estimated
from Statistics of Major Trading Partners, 1950–68**
(computed from f.o.b. values in U.S. dollars)

Year	Exports	Imports	Year	Exports	Imports
1950	101.7	n.a.	1960	93.6	93.8
1951	97.2	n.a.	1961	86.3	89.1
1952	98.1	n.a.	1962	90.2	95.3
1953	98.3	n.a.	1963	101.7	82.9
1954	94.4	99.1	1964	98.7	90.8
1955	92.5	101.7	1965	99.0	87.3
1956	91.3	92.9	1966	94.0	87.6
1957	85.2	92.3	1967	89.7	87.4
1958	102.8	98.2	1968	91.5	89.0
1959	100.1	91.4			

n.a. = not available.

SOURCE: George L. Hicks, "Philippine Foreign Trade, 1950–1965: Basic Data and Major Characteristics" and "Philippine Foreign Trade Statistics: Supplementary Data and Interpretations, 1954–1966" (Washington, D.C.: National Planning Association, Center for Development Planning, 1967; mimeo.), except for 1966–68 which are from George L. Hicks and Geoffrey McNicoll, *Trade and Growth in the Philippines* (Ithaca: Cornell University Press, 1971), p. 46.

Japan, as reported by the Japanese government, were $36 million.[25] A similar extensive degree of undervaluation also existed in 1966.

To test the hypothesis that the degree of import undervaluation is positively related to the height of duty levied on an item, a comparison was made of 1967 f.o.b. import values, supplied by the Philippine Central Bank, and f.o.b. export values of the same items, from the U.S. Department of Commerce, for a sample of 62 commodities. The resulting regression equation was $y = -1.65 + 14.70x$, where y = ratio of U.S. data on U.S. exports to the Philippines to Philippine data on Philippine imports from the United States, and x = 1969 ad valorem percentage tariff rates in the Philippines. The t value for the coefficient of x is 4.27, which is significant at the 1 per cent level, and the coefficient of correlation (r) is 0.48. Thus, the hypothesis that the higher the tariff the greater the degree of undervaluation is supported by the statistical analysis. Moreover, the degree of undervaluation increases very sharply as the duty rises.

In addition to commodities being imported without the payment of import taxes because of open or technical smuggling, many dutiable items are imported without being taxed because of legal exemptions. Imports of capital goods in industries registered with the Board of Investment have already been mentioned in Chapter 3. Exemptions of this sort are deliberately designed to foster growth in high-priority industries. Other sectors, organizations, or items that are specifically exempted from certain import taxes for reasons of growth, employment, or equity include fertilizer manufacturers, the textile industry, the petroleum industry, private development banks, agricultural cooperatives, cottage industries, government entities, the National Power Corporation, the National Waterworks and Sewerage Authority, the Philippine National Railways, Philippine Airlines, various electric authorities, the Philippine Virginia Tobacco Association, the Rice and Corn Administration, the National Marketing Authority, personal effects of foreign residents, and donations from abroad to local charitable, religious, and civic organizations. As the customs commissioner has pointed out, goods normally taxed that are imported under special tax-exemption laws frequently are not used for the purpose for which the exemption is granted but, instead, find their way into regular market channels.[26]

As long as some import flows continue through proper channels, domestic prices will be unaffected by the various measures described above to avoid import taxes.[27] Rather than being hurt by a decrease in protection, domestic producers are adversely affected mainly through a loss of markets because of these various illegal activities. However, there also are many dutiable items in the Philippine import statistics on which no import duties are collected because of legal exemptions. In these cases not only do domestic producers lose markets to smugglers and others who illegally channel goods into commercial markets, but also the price of the product is depressed by these activities. The height of the tariff and other taxes on imports then incorrectly measures the protection given local producers. How important this point is for measuring the general contours of Philippine protectionism is not known.

Another important effect of an overvalued exchange rate is to increase the use of imported capital goods by local producers. Since capital goods imports are favored by exchange authorities, importers find that it is easy to make windfall gains by transferring funds abroad through overinvoiced purchases of these items. The highly specialized nature of most of these items makes overinvoicing hard to detect, and the ability to borrow at below-market interest rates makes this activity doubly attractive. In a scenario common in the Philippines, high protection plus subsidized loans and guarantees are provided for a potential import-competing activity; later, it is discovered that the high duty encourages so much smuggling of various sorts that the market left is too small to take advantage of all the economies of scale. Excess capacity develops because the capital goods are purchased in expectation of a larger market than in fact materializes. In addition, some producer-importers apparently have no intention of trying to run a successful business. Instead, they arrange with foreign exporters to overreport the value of their capital goods imports and thereby transfer some of the borrowed funds to accounts abroad. They are unable to repay the funds borrowed from such organizations as the Development Bank of the Philippines, but still end up with the funds transferred abroad as a gain. However, inflated capital-output ratios and excess capacity are the price that the country as a whole pays.[28]

SUMMARY

All the measures of protection analyzed in this chapter bring out essentially the same story. Beginning in 1950 and 1951 the Philippine government undertook a policy of sharply curtailing imports of consumption goods in order to favor the importation of the raw materials and capital goods needed for industrial development. This is very apparent from the behavior of the various EERs as well as the EPRs, all of which indicate a sharp increase in the protection of nonessential goods relative to essential goods and exports in 1951. The import-cutback program coupled with the economic prosperity associated with the Korean War caused the implicit protection on essential consumption goods to rise more than the government wished, but by 1953 the government seemed to have mastered the technique of providing high protection to nonessential goods while still permitting liberal imports of essential consumer and producer goods.

For the rest of the 1950s, beginning with 1953, when the Central Bank became the sole manager of the system of import and exchange controls, the protection and subsidization provided to domestic industries producing nonessential consumer and producer goods continued to widen relative to the production of essential commodities and export products. Protective rates for a number of nonessential consumer goods seem to have doubled during the 1950s. Of particular significance is that the domestic purchasing power of a given quantity of exports declined steadily in those years.

The dismantling of the exchange-control system during the early 1960s did not represent a significant liberalization in the sense of sharply reducing the differences in production incentives among the various import sectors. For example, in 1963, the real effective exchange rate, i.e., the PPP-EER, of imported nonessential consumer items was 2.65 times as large as that for imported essential consumer goods, and the PPP-EER for nonessential producer goods was 1.52 times as large as that for essential producer goods. These figures are higher than the same ratios in 1959, although the 1959 figures do not include any scarcity premiums due to exchange controls. The gap in incentives between traditional exports and import-competing sectors also remained high.

From 1963 through 1969 the relative protection between essential and nonessential consumer goods as well as between essential and nonessential producer goods remained the same. However, the real cost of imports in absolute terms declined somewhat between 1963 and 1969. Nevertheless, this cost was still between 1.7 and 5.0 times larger than in 1949. One encouraging development after 1963 was the shift in incentives in favor of firms producing new exports. Between 1963 and 1969 the PPP-EER for new exports increased in contrast to the general decline for import transactions. However, this rate still remained low compared to those in the import-competing sectors.

The 1970 exchange crisis brought about further substantial increases in both nominal and real effective exchange rates. These rates declined somewhat in 1971 but were still at record heights. To sustain an economic expansion by foreign borrowing, much of it of a short-term, limited nature, it was eventually necessary to raise the real domestic costs of importing and again to shift production incentives in favor of exporters.

APPENDIX: CALCULATING EFFECTIVE EXCHANGE RATES AND EFFECTIVE RATES OF PROTECTION

Data Used in Calculating Effective Exchange Rates, by Exchange-Control Category, 1949–71.

EXCHANGE RATES

The EER for a particular exchange-control category and year is obtained by increasing (decreasing) the applicable official exchange rate by the various trade taxes (subsidies) that must be paid on transactions of this type. The exchange rates (in terms of number of pesos per U.S. dollar) used in the calculations are as follows:

1949–59—P2.00 for all groups;

1960—essential consumer goods and essential producer goods, including those for "new and necessary" industries, P2.08; semiessential producer goods, P2.10; traditional and new exports, P2.22; nonessential consumer goods, semiessential consumer goods, and nonessential producer goods, P2.83;

1961—essential consumer goods and essential producer goods, including those for "new and necessary" industries, P2.92; semiessential producer goods, P2.93; nonessential consumer goods, semiessential consumer goods, and nonessential producer goods, P3.0; traditional and new exports, P2.68;

1962—all groups except traditional and new exports, P3.44; traditional and new exports, P3.15;

1963–69—all groups except traditional exports and new exports, P3.90;

1963–64—traditional and new exports, P3.52;

1965–69—traditional and new exports, P3.90;

1970—all groups except traditional exports, P5.89; traditional exports (taking account of the 80-20 split between the old and new exchange rate), P5.57;

1971—all groups P6.40.

TARIFFS

From 1946 to 1955, when a free-trade arrangement was in effect between the United States and the Philippines, no duty is included. From 1956 to 1971, the nominal duty levels in the Philippines were multiplied by the following percentages in order to reflect the increasing proportion of the nominal duty that was applicable against U.S. goods: 1956–58, 25 per cent; 1959–61, 50 per cent; 1962–64, 75 per cent; 1965–73, 90 per cent. The nominal tariff rates used for the various categories are shown in the accompanying table.

	1956	*1957–61*	*1962–71*
Consumer goods			
Nonessential	18%	51%	83%
Semiessential	35	40	40
Essential	15	12	9
Producer goods			
Nonessential	20	25	100
Semiessential	15	22	29
Essential	22	22	25

Producer goods for "new and necessary industries"—same as for essential producer goods.

EXCISE TAX AND MARGIN FEE ON SALE OF FOREIGN EXCHANGE

For all groups except essential consumer goods and producer goods for new industries (both of which were exempted from these charges): 1951–54, 17 per cent; 1955–58, zero; 1959, 25 per cent; 1960, 24 per cent; 1961, 16 per cent; 1962–71, zero.

SPECIAL IMPORT TAX

For 1949–54, zero; 1955–56, 17 per cent; 1957, 15.3 per cent; 1958, 13.6 per cent; 1959, 11.9 per cent; 1960, 10.2 per cent; 1961, 8.5 per cent;

1962, 6.8 per cent; 1963, 5.1 per cent; 1964, 3.4 per cent; 1965, 1.7 per cent; 1966–71, zero. (Exemptions are the same as above.)

PROTECTIVE EFFECT OF SALES OR COMPENSATING TAX

The discriminatory aspect of the sales tax on imports arises because the base on which the tax is levied is greater than that for domestically produced commodities and also because the sales tax was levied not only on the import duty, but also on the special import tax in effect from 1955–65. The protective effect of the sales tax was determined by multiplying the sales tax rate by the sum of 1 plus the special import tax rate plus the tariff rate on U.S. imports, and then multiplying this product by the sum of 1 plus the rate by which the import valuation base exceeded the valuation base for comparable domestic goods. The sales tax rate was then deducted from this result to obtain the net discriminatory effect.

The sales tax rates for the various commodity groups are as follows. Nonessential consumer goods: 1949, 30 per cent; 1950–71, 50 per cent; semiessential consumer goods, essential consumer goods, nonessential producer goods, semiessential producer goods, and essential producer goods: 1949–50, zero; 1951–71, 7 per cent. The special import tax rate and the relevant tariff rates have already been given in this appendix. The size of the valuation base for imports as compared to domestically produced goods is as follows: nonessential consumer goods—1949–50, 1; 1951–71, 2; semiessential and essential consumer goods—1949–50, 1; 1951–71, 1.25; nonessential and semiessential producer goods—1949–50, 1; 1951–71, 1.25; essential producer goods—1949–50, 1; 1951–71, 1.25; essential producer goods for "new and necessary" industries—1949–71, exempt from the tax.

MARGIN-DEPOSIT REQUIREMENTS

Estimates of the protective effect of the various margin requirements for importing are shown in Table 5-12.

SUBSIDY ON NEW EXPORTS

In estimating the net subsidy for producing new export commodities, it was assumed that such industries could borrow from government organizations such as the Development Bank of the Philippines at 2 per cent below the market rate. Assuming an incremental capital-output ratio of 2, this implies a 4 per cent subsidy on output. For the 1949–62 period, the subsidy effect of the various tax exemptions for these industries was taken from a study by the Philippine Chamber of Commerce, reported in *Official Proceedings,* Fifth Annual Convention of Manufacturers and Producers, Volume VIII, 1958; for the period thereafter, it was estimated from a sample of firms analyzed by the Board of Investment. The figures used are as follows: 1949–52, 8.2 per

TABLE 5-12

Protective Effects of Margin-Deposit Requirements, 1949–71

(per cent)

	1949–53	1954–57	1958	1959	1960–61	1962–65	1966	1967	1968	1969	1970	1971
Consumer goods												
Nonessential	2.4	0	6	3	0	4.0	0	2.25	5.7	6.5	6.0	1.5
Semiessential	2.4	0	6	3	0	2.25	0	1.1	3.1	3.25	0.6	1.5
Essential[a]												
Producer goods												
Nonessential	2.4	0	3	3	0	2.25	0	1.12	2.25	3.25	0.6	1.5
Semiessential	0	0	3	3	0	0.75	0	0.75	2.25	2.44	0.6	1.5
Essential	0	0	3	3	0	0	0	0.37	1.32	0.78	0	0
For "new and necessary" industries	0	0	1.5	1.5	0	0	0	0	0	0	0	0

a. The rate was zero throughout the period shown.

cent; 1953–58, 12.1 per cent; 1959, 10.9 per cent; 1960, 9.1 per cent; 1961, 6.1 per cent; 1962, 3 per cent; 1963–66, 2 per cent; 1967–69, 3 per cent; 1970–71, 7 per cent.

TAX ON TRADITIONAL EXPORTS

An export tax of 10 per cent was levied on traditional exports beginning in May 1970. The tax was continued in 1971.

Calculation of Effective Rates of Protection by Exchange-Control Category, 1949–71.

The commodities included in each group are the same as those included in the estimates of EERs by exchange-control category. The protection (penalty or subsidy in the case of exports) on the output of a particular import category for a specific year is equal to the percentage by which the EER in that category exceeds the EER for producer goods used by "new and necessary" industries in that year. The protection on inputs for all categories except semiessential producer goods after 1956, producer goods for "new and necessary" industries, and new exports is assumed to equal the degree of protection on essential producer goods. For semiessential producer goods after 1956, the protective rate on inputs is the same as the protective rate on essential producer goods except for the tariff component of this protection. For 1962–71 the duty component is the duty on inputs into aqua ammonia as reported by Valdepeñas,[29] namely, 4.4 per cent. For 1957–61, 3.9 per cent is used as the duty component of the protective rate on inputs.

The protection on inputs used in "new and necessary" industries and for new exports is assumed to be zero.

The formula for the effective rate of protection is

$$\frac{t_j - \Sigma a_{ij} t_i}{1 - \Sigma a_{ij}},$$

where t_j is the tariff rate on any output, t_i is the tariff rate on any output used as an input in the production of the jth output, and a_{ij} is the value of the ith output used to produce a unit value of the jth output at free-trade prices. The various a_{ij} coefficients also are based on data from Valdepeñas.[30] His tariff-inclusive a_{ij}s are corrected to obtain free-trade a_{ij}s and then combined to obtain unweighted averages of these coefficients for the appropriate categories. The averages are as follows: nonessential consumer goods, 0.47; semiessential consumer goods, 0.39; essential consumer goods, 0.35; nonessential producer goods, 0.56; semiessential producer goods, 0.19; essential producer goods, 0.50; producer goods for "new and necessary" industries, 0.50; traditional exports, 0.44; new exports, 0.48.

NOTES

1. Estimates of domestic resource costs—which is a measure of the value of domestic resources (at opportunity cost prices) employed in earning or saving a dollar of foreign exchange (in the value-added sense) when a good is produced domestically—are not included in this study, although such estimates were made for other country studies in the series of which this study is a part. Underlying Philippine data did not seem sufficiently extensive or accurate to warrant including these DRC estimates.

2. See Appendix A for definitions of the various concepts employed in the project of which this study is a part.

3. Since imports from the United States were so significant, especially during the years when tariff preferences were substantial, the tariff rates used in calculating effective exchange rates in these tables are those applicable to imports from the United States, i.e., they take account of the tariff preferences extended to American goods. In 1950, for example, imports from the United States amounted to 75 per cent of all Philippine imports. This percentage had fallen to 42 per cent by 1960 and 29 per cent by 1970.

4. See Vicente B. Valdepeñas, Jr., *The Protection and Development of Philippine Manufacturing* (Manila: Ateneo University Press, 1970), Table 6.1, pp. 82–85, for a listing of these commodities.

5. See loc. cit. for a listing of these commodities.

6. Valdepeñas's choice of sample was influenced by his objective of obtaining detailed information on duties for inputs used in producing various goods. He was able to obtain such information from confidential files of the Tariff Commission that were assembled in response to requests for tariff changes after the devaluation of 1962. Since requests and studies for tariff changes tend to occur for items for which there is an above-average chance of a tariff increase, Valdepeñas's sample tends to exaggerate the tariff increases classified by essentiality categories after 1962. This is confirmed by an analysis of all tariff changes between 1957 and 1970 classified by standard commodity groups. This upward bias could be especially misleading in the essential-producer-goods class, and a more representative item was therefore picked for the post-1962 period. The upward bias is also present, it should be noted, in the nonessential goods category (where a correction is not made for the post-1962 period), but it appears that duties were in fact raised on a larger proportion of all items in this group than on the essential-producer-goods group.

7. Two difficulties with tracing EERs over time are the shift of items from one exchange-control category to another and the establishment of new categories. Thermos bottles, for example, are included among the 32 items in Valdepeñas's list of nonessential consumer goods, which is based on the 1953 classification of imports by the Ceneral Bank. When the semiessential category was created, in 1957, this item was transferred out of the nonessential-consumer-goods class.

8. Loudspeakers were also classified as a nonessential consumer good, and aqua ammonia as a nonessential producer good, in the 1953 classification system.

9. The list of goods in this category narrowed over time as more producer goods were produced locally with the aid of a high degree of protection.

10. The 1959 EERs for the types of goods mentioned in this paragraph were computed as follows. The average tariff for the sample of goods included in the nonessential-consumer-goods group was 51 per cent in 1959. Since U.S. goods were subject to only 50 per cent of the duty in that year, the cost-increasing effect of the tariff was $0.5 \times 0.51 \times P2.00 = P0.51$. The 25 per cent margin fee and the special import tax, which had

decreased to 11.9 per cent, added P0.74, i.e. $(0.25 + 0.119) \times$ P2.00, to the official peso cost of a dollar's worth of goods. The sales tax further increased the cost of importing, since, as noted in the appendix to this chapter, it was required that the 50 per cent tax be levied on twice the cost of imports. Whereas the sales tax on a domestically produced nonessential consumer good costing 2 pesos was 1 peso, the tax on a comparable imported good was $0.5 \times (1.000 + 0.374) \times$ P2.00 $\times 2.0 =$ P2.748, or P1.748 more than the domestic good. Finally, the required margin deposit of 100 per cent (assumed to be for a three-month period and at a forgone annual interest rate of 12 per cent) added 3 per cent, or $0.03 \times$ P2.00 = P0.06 to the official cost of a dollar's worth of imports. In total, these measures added P3.06 $(0.51 + 0.74 + 1.75 + 0.06)$ to the official P2.00 cost of a dollar and brought the EER to P5.06 per dollar for nonessential consumer goods. Imports of essential consumer goods, on the other hand, were impaired only by a modest tariff (6 per cent) and a 2.3 per cent discriminatory effect from the sales tax. The EER per dollar for this category of imports was, therefore $(0.06 + 0.023) \times$ P2.00 + P2.00 = P2.17. Imports of producer goods for "new and necessary" industries were exempt from all charges except the margin-deposit requirement, and the EER in 1959 was P2.03 per dollar. The value of the internal tax exemptions for new export industries was 10.9 per cent in that year, and the interest subsidy on output was assumed to remain at 4 per cent throughout the period (see the appendix to this chapter). This 14.9 per cent subsidy on sales yields a figure of P2.30 per dollar for the EER for new exports, i.e., 1.149 $\times$ P2.00.

11. The actual shifts in the structure of production are analyzed in the next chapter.

12. Again, it should be noted that this figure is an underestimate of the increase in the market cost of imports because of the existence of exchange controls in 1959.

13. The explicit rate of protection is taken to be the percentage by which the EER for a particular category exceeds the EER for producer goods for "new and necessary" industries.

14. The Central Bank stopped publishing import unit values by detailed commodity groups after 1955.

15. Let x be the 1951 c.i.f. prices of nonessential goods, $2x$ the implicit protection on these goods, and $3.0x$ the 1951 domestic price. Since this price increased 0.8 between 1951 and 1959, the 1959 price is $5.4x$. Dividing this by x, the 1959 c.i.f. price, gives 5.4 or 440 per cent $[(5.4 - 1.0) \times 100]$ as the rate of protection in 1959. Changes in c.i.f. import unit values are not taken into account in the calculation, since this index actually declined slightly between 1951 and 1959.

16. The steps in the calculation are as follows: (a) The peso cost of a dollar's worth of nonessential consumer goods in 1962 was 1.98 times as large as in 1959, i.e., 10.04/5.06, whereas the import unit value (in dollars) index in 1962 was 1.04 times its 1959 level. The peso cost of a given bundle of nonessential consumer goods in 1962 was, therefore, $1.98 \times 1.04 = 2.06$ times its 1959 cost. Put the other way around, the peso cost of a given bundle of nonessential consumer goods in 1959 was 1.00/2.06 or 0.49 of its 1962 level. (b) Since the wholesale price index for nonessential consumer goods was 308 in 1962 (Table 5-6) when there were no exchange controls and thus no windfall profits, the cost of these goods in 1959 including the effects of all fiscal and monetary measures and expressed in terms of the wholesale price index was 151, i.e., 0.49×308. (c) Thus, the c.i.f. cost of these goods in 1959 equaled 151 less the effects of the fiscal and monetary measures. Since the effects of these measures provided a protective rate of 149 per cent, the c.i.f. import cost expressed in terms of the wholesale price index was 61, i.e., letting x be the c.i.f. import cost, $1.49x + x = 151$. (d) Because the cost in terms of the wholesale price index was 61 in 1959 while the actual wholesale price index

in 1959 was 281 (Table 5-6), the level of implicit protection in that year was [(281/61) − 1] × 100 = 361 per cent.

17. This figure would be the implicit rate in 1959 because the wholesale price of the product was the same in 1959 as in 1951.

18. John H. Power, "The Structure of Protection in the Philippines," in Bela Balassa and associates, *The Structure of Protection in Developing Countries* (Baltimore: Johns Hopkins Press, 1971), pp. 271–280. Input-output data for the manufacturing sector were obtained by Power from the 1965 Survey of Manufactures, made available by the Philippine Bureau of Census and Statistics, whereas input-output data for nonmanufacturing sectors were based on the Philippine Census of Manufactures for 1961.

19. It appears, however, that Power's correction for the discriminatory effect of the sales tax is excessive. He compares the tax levied on the marked-up value of imports with the tax levied domestically on "the portion of the manufacturer's price that represents inputs not already taxed (for the most part, value-added plus electricity, fuel, and depreciation)" (Power, "Protection in the Philippines," p. 271). While it is true that a particular domestic manufacturer pays on this base, the prices of previously taxed inputs are already inflated, and they cut into the protection on value added. His measure of the degree of preference provided domestic producers would be correct only if no tax had been levied on these inputs. However, except for such items as automobiles, jewelry, toilet preparations, sporting goods, refrigerators, synthetics, silk and wool fabrics, television sets, combination radio and phonograph sets, luggage, and furniture, where the sales tax is between 30 and 50 per cent and the markup between 50 and 100 per cent, the exaggeration of the protective effect of the sales tax by Power is not very significant. The sales tax for most nonluxury items is only 7 per cent; and the markup on imports, 25 per cent. Thus, for a commodity for which value added plus electricity and fuel amounts to 40 per cent of its total value, the exaggeration of the implicit import tax would amount to only five percentage points.

20. The 97-sector, input-output transaction table for 1965 together with tariff and sales-tax data were kindly supplied by Tito A. Mijares, the director of the Philippine Bureau of the Census and Statistics.

21. See the appendix to the chapter for the source of these data.

22. In 1958 and 1959 the lowest rate for imports was P2.03 to the dollar.

23. Cited by F. H. Golay, *The Philippines: Public Policy and National Economic Development* (Ithaca: Cornell University Press, 1961), p. 151.

24. In the case of imports, however, it is suggested by the data in Table 5-11 that the incentive to overvalue imports as a means of shifting funds abroad was outweighed by smuggling and by the incentive to undervalue the goods in order to reduce customs duties.

25. E. B. Ayal, *The Philippine Cotton Textile Industry* (Center for Development Planning, National Planning Association, Field Work Report 24, January 1968).

26. *Central Bank News Digest,* August 31, 1971, p. 5.

27. It is assumed that foreign prices are the same regardless of the volume of Philippine imports.

28. For a discussion of the welfare effects of smuggling, see J. Bhagwati and B. Hansen, "A Theoretical Analysis of Smuggling," *Quarterly Journal of Economics,* May 1973.

29. *Philippine Manufacturing.*

30. Ibid., Table 6.2, pp. 91–96.

Chapter 6

Effects of Philippine Trade and Development Policies on Resource Allocation, Growth, and Income Distribution

After a brief outline had been given of the various phases of exchange control through which the Philippine economy has passed during the last twenty-five years, a detailed description was presented, in Chapters 2, 3, and 4, of both the trade and payments policies and monetary and fiscal policies followed by the country during that period. An attempt was then made, in Chapter 5, to quantify the differential levels of protection that these combined policies afforded to various sectors of the economy. In the present chapter, the study is concluded by analyzing the effects of the different exchange-control methods and other development policies on the industrial allocation of resources, the distribution of income, and the rate of growth in the economy.

RESOURCE-ALLOCATION EFFECTS

Evidence on changes in the pattern of production within the Philippines is consistent with the hypothesis that the differential incentives associated with the exchange-control and other protective policies pursued by the government did contribute to both an acceleration of the industrialization process during the 1950s and a diversification of manufacturing activities. On the other hand, the effectiveness of export activities in attracting productive resources tended to be undermined during this period, thereby inhibiting continuation of the kind of industrialization program that had been undertaken.

121

Manufacturing.

As is evident from Table 6-1, which contains Hooley's calculations of growth rates and the composition of output from the turn of the century to

TABLE 6-1

Gross Value Added in Agriculture, Manufacturing, and
Other Nonagricultural Activities, 1902–61

Year	Percentage Distribution			Annual Growth Rates (compounded)[a]			
	Agri.	Mfg.	Other Nonagri.	Agri.	Mfg.	Other Nonagri.	Total
1902	55.0	13.0	32.0				
1918	60.4	12.3	27.3	5.4	3.8	3.5	4.7
1928	53.7	16.3[b]	30.0[b]	0.7	4.7	2.7	1.9
1938	46.6	21.2	32.2	0.5	4.6	2.7	1.9
1948	49.1	17.5	33.4	0	−2.3	−0.2	−0.5
1961	33.6	28.0	38.4	3.8	10.9	8.1	6.8

SOURCE: Richard W. Hooley, "Long-Term Economic Growth in the Philippines, 1902–1961," in "Growth of Output in the Philippines" (Papers presented at a conference of the International Rice Research Institute, Los Baños, Laguna, December 9–10, 1966; mimeo.). Hooley's Tables 1 and 3 were used in preparing the data shown.

a. The growth rates refer to the period between the year for which the rate is listed and the previously listed year.

b. Since for 1928 Hooley does not break down the share of nonagricultural activities in gross value added into its manufacturing and nonmanufacturing components, the averages in 1918 and 1938 of these components are applied to the 1928 share of all nonagricultural activities in gross value added.

1961, the shift toward manufacturing and other nonagricultural activities during the 1950s should be regarded as the continuation of an established trend rather than as an entirely new development. Indeed, it seems reasonable that a significant share of the rapid growth in manufacturing during the 1950s was part of the kind of "catch-up" growth that one would expect in view of the stagnation and destruction during the wartime years. For example, not only was gross value added in manfacturing in 1948 still 21 per cent below its prewar level, but the population of the country was 20 per cent greater in 1948 than 1939. Nevertheless, the rate of growth of manufacturing between 1948 and 1961 was 2.3 times greater than in the best decade of manufacturing growth of the 1902–48 period, suggesting that the strong economic incentives offered to most industrial sectors after World War II contributed to a quickening of industrial growth.

What is more evident than the impact of trade and payments policies on the over-all growth rate in manufacturing is the effect that these policies had on increasing the degree of diversification in manufacturing. This diversification is brought out in Table 6-2, which contains estimates of the distribution of activities within the manufacturing sector from 1902 to 1970. From 1918 to 1948, the food, beverages, and tobacco sector accounted for between 60 and 65 per cent of all value added in the manufacturing sector. However, between 1948 and 1956, the share of this sector dropped to 44 per cent, with such industries as textiles, chemicals, basic metals, machinery, transportation, and miscellaneous manufactures showing significant increases. From 1956 to 1965, the share of food, beverages, and tobacco declined only moderately, to 40 per cent, although there were important shifts within the other sectors of manufacturing. The machinery and transport equipment industries, for example, grew from 4.3 per cent of all manufacturing activity in 1956 to 7.6 per cent in 1965. Between 1965 and 1970 the food, beverages, and tobacco share again dropped significantly, to 34.7 per cent, while the machinery and transport equipment share rose to 10.4 per cent.

As was pointed out in Chapter 2, the main means of stimulating domestic production in both new and old manufacturing lines was to protect local industries from import competition and thus shift domestic demand away from foreign goods and toward domestically produced substitutes. That import substitution occurred on a widespread basis, especially between 1948 and 1956, as is evident from Table 6-3. The ratio of imports of all manufacturers to the gross value of manufacturing output fell from 1.13 to 0.55 between 1948 and 1956, and then declined more slowly, reaching 0.42 by 1968. The same sharp decline in imports relative to domestic production during the early 1950s is seen in the data for a selected list of commodities in Table 6-4.

The government's protection policy was guided throughout the two decades by the principle that importation of basic necessities consumed by low-income groups and of essential intermediate and producer goods should be as liberal as possible, provided they could not be produced domestically except at very high costs. Industries involving relatively simple processing activities that gave some promise of being able to produce on a reasonably efficient basis were given tax assistance as "new and necessary" industries and were also aided by very tight import restrictions. Many production lines that could not be regarded as "new and necessary" even under a very liberal interpretation of this phrase did, nevertheless, benefit from high levels of protection designed to free foreign exchange for imports of essential consumer and producer

TABLE 6-2

Distribution of Value Added of Philippine Manufacturing
by Industry Groups,[a] 1902–70
(per cent)

ISIC Code	Industry	1902	1918	1938	1948	1956	1960	1965	1970
20–22	Food manufacturing, beverages, and tobacco products	62.6	65.8	64.0	60.6	43.8	41.2	40.1	34.7
23	Textile products	0.5	0.5	0.8	2.6	3.7	4.6	4.7	5.6
24	Footwear and other wearing apparel	5.9	3.5	7.8	6.6	5.1	3.0	7.0	4.3
25	Wood and cork products	8.0	5.4	5.3	9.7	5.0	4.0	4.6	4.4
26	Furniture and fixtures	2.3	1.3	1.9	1.8	1.3	0.9	1.4	0.9
27	Paper and paper products	0.0	0.0	0.0	0.0	1.7	2.3	2.1	2.9
28	Printing and printed products	4.9	1.7	3.6	3.7	3.1	3.2	4.1	2.7
29	Leather products	0.7	0.3	0.1	0.0	0.2	0.3	0.3	0.3
30	Rubber products	0.0	0.0	0.0	0.6	0.9	3.2	2.9	4.0
31	Chemicals and chemical products	1.9	10.9	6.9	2.9	9.9	10.0	9.1	9.9
32	Products of coal and petroleum	b	b	c	c	c	c	c	c
33	Nonmetallic mineral products	3.9	0.7	3.3	2.1	4.7	3.7	4.4	3.7
34, 35	Basic metal and metallic products	0.9	0.8	0.7	1.9	4.7	8.0	6.5	8.9
36, 37	Machinery	3.6	0.8	0.2	0.5	2.1	4.2	4.8	6.9
38	Transportation equipment	b	1.3	0.4	1.0	2.2	2.2	2.8	3.5
39	Miscellaneous manufactures	4.2	5.9	3.9	5.7	11.2	8.2	5.2	7.3
	Total manufacturing	100.0	100.0	100.0	100.0	100.0	100.0	100.0	100.0

ISIC = International Standard Industrial Classification.

SOURCE: 1902–60—Salvador C. Umaña, "Growth of Output of Philippine Manufacturing: 1902–1960," in "Growth of Output in the Philippines" (Papers presented at a conference of the International Rice Research Institute, Los Baños, Laguna, December 9–10, 1966; mimeo.); 1965 and 1970—National Economic Council, *Statistical Reporter*, January–March 1969 and April–June 1971.

a. For 1902–60, 1938 prices; 1965 and 1970 at current prices.

b. Negligible.

c. Included in miscellaneous manufactures.

goods. To this extent, the effect of the policies was to divert scarce resources into nonessential uses.

There was comparatively little scope for import substitution in the food field, since the ratio of imports to production in this industry was already relatively low in 1948. Moreover, the industry included many essential consumer goods and export products—commodities whose production was not encouraged by the structure of protection. For example, products of rice and corn mills were classified as essential consumer goods, whereas coconut oil, desiccated coconut, and sugar were export products. These four products alone accounted for more than 75 per cent of the total output of the food products sector and nearly 50 per cent of the total value of all manufactures. Another factor preventing an increase in the relative importance of sugar production was the U.S. import quota on this item. Thus, it is not surprising that import substitution was comparatively modest in the food field and that this sector declined sharply in relative importance as a manufacturing activity in the country.

For similar reasons, import substitution was slight in the furniture and fixtures and wood and cork products industries. On the other hand, in fields such as textiles and leather products, the extent of import substitution between 1948 and 1968 was considerable both because imports were still very important in 1948 and because these were relatively simple industries that were prime candidates for protectionist efforts. Imports were also comparatively large in 1948 in such areas as chemicals, metal products, machinery, and transportation equipment. Though the production of many items in these industries was far too costly for the country to undertake under its import-substitution goals, there were also many commodities in these sectors that could be produced under subsidies granted by various protectionist devices without unduly raising input costs in the industrial sector. These were mainly nonessential consumption commodities or simply produced capital goods.

This trend toward the production of nonessential consumer goods is evident when one examines the detailed manufacturing structure of the country in 1960.[1] Rapid growth occurred between 1948 and 1960 in such nonessential industries as the assembly of motor vehicles, electrical household appliances of various sorts, household radios, phonographs, and television sets, as well as the production of toilet preparations and paper stationery. These are the kinds of industries that sprang up in response to the very high levels of protection placed on nonessential consumer goods. The Central Bank could, of course, have blocked the importation of producer goods necessary to establish these industries, but it did not. One indication of the high degree of protection afforded to almost all the industries in the manufacturing sector is that 80 of the 102 four-digit products included in the 1960 Census of Manufactures were listed in that year by the Central Bank as either unclassified items (importable

TABLE 6-3

Measurement of Import Substitution in Manufacturing in the Philippines, 1948, 1956, 1960, and 1968

ISIC Code	Industry	Gross Value of Production (total manufacturing in millions of current pesos; distribution by industry in percentages of total)				Value of Imports, f.o.b.				Ratio of Value of Imports to Value of Production			
		1948	1956	1960	1968	1949[a]	1956	1960	1968	1948 to 1949[a]	1956	1960	1968
	Total manufacturing	1,040	1,842	3,244	10,723	1,172	1,012	1,371	4,486	1.13	0.55	0.42	0.42
20	Food, manufactured	68.1	26.4	26.5	23.7	25.3	17.4	14.0	11.5	0.47	0.24	0.16	0.15
21	Beverages		7.8	6.5	5.8	3.4	1.4	0.1	0.8				
22	Tobacco products		8.0	5.5	5.5			0.01					
23	Textiles	3.4	5.9	8.0	7.1	19.2	11.8	5.0	3.8	6.32	1.11	0.27	0.22
24	Footwear and other wearing apparel	5.9[b]	6.5	3.3	1.7	2.4	0.3	0.2	0.1	0.46	0.02[d]	0.02[d]	0.02[d]
25	Wood and cork products	13.3	5.6	4.5	5.1	0.3	0.4	0.1	0.04	0.03	0.01	0.01	0.01
26	Furniture and fixtures		0.9	0.6	0.4	0.03	0.02	0.01	0.1				
27	Paper and paper products	0.1	2.0	3.3	2.9	3.0	3.6	2.8	2.4	43.79	0.98	0.35	0.35
28	Printing and printed products	2.0	2.8	2.3	1.9	0.9	n.a.	n.a.	n.a.	0.53	n.a.	n.a.	n.a.
29	Leather and leather products	0.1	0.3	0.4	0.3	0.9	0.7	0.4	0.05	11.60	1.22	0.35	0.07
30	Rubber products	[c]	0.9	3.3	2.4	2.0	2.9	0.6	0.6	n.a.	1.65	0.07	0.11
31, 32	Chemicals and petroleum products	1.5	12.3	12.4	14.4	11.9	7.7	9.0	9.5	8.76	0.34	0.31	0.28
33	Nonmetallic mineral products	1.4	3.9	3.1	3.6	2.2	3.0	1.1	1.0	1.73	0.22	0.15	0.12
34	Basic metal products	n.a.	0.8	1.6	2.9	n.a.	15.2	2.3	2.8	n.a.	10.26	2.12	0.61
35	Fabricated metal products	2.8	3.9	5.8	4.9	4.7	3.0	2.3	3.7	6.98	0.41	0.17	0.32
36	Machinery except electrical		0.8	0.8	1.3	5.0	15.2	14.3	20.7		10.26	7.65	6.76
37	Electrical machinery		0.8	2.7	3.1	2.9	3.8	3.5	5.3		2.65	0.56	0.71
38	Transportation equipment		2.8	2.9	5.2	4.9	5.7	18.2	12.5		1.12	2.66	1.01
39	Miscellaneous manufactures	1.4	7.7	6.6	7.9	5.5	3.1	3.1	3.7	4.38	0.22	0.19	0.20

Notes to Table 6-3

ISIC = International Standard Industrial Classification.

n.a. = not available.

SOURCE: Data on imports from Central Bank of the Philippines, *Statistical Bulletin*, December 1969; and United Nations, *Yearbook of International Trade Statistics*, 1953 and 1956. Data on gross value of production from Philippine Bureau of Census and Statistics, *Annual Survey of Manufactures: 1956*, vol. 1 (Manila: Bureau of Printing, 1958); ibid., *1960*, vol. 5 (1962); ibid., *1968*, Preliminary Report; and United Nations, *The Growth of World Industry, 1938–1961: National Tables* (1963).

a. Trade data for 1949 are used with 1948 production data because the Central Bank's series on imports does not begin until 1949. Since imports in 1949 were almost the same as in 1948, i.e., \$586 million versus \$593 million, and the import control program was not effective until 1950, this should not bias the import-substitution results.

b. Includes industries 24 and 30.

c. Included in industry 24.

d. The ratio of imports to gross value of production for industries 24 and 30 combined was 0.23 in 1956, 0.32 in 1960, and 0.07 in 1968.

TABLE 6-4

Production and Imports of Selected Commodities, 1948, 1953, 1954, and 1956
(pesos in thousands)

	Production	Imports	Ratio: Imports to Production	Production	Imports	Ratio: Imports to Production
		——1948——			——1954——	
Cigars and cigarettes	P17,061	P47,680	2.79	P147,384	P 3,600	0.02
Soap	13,720	4,865	0.35	26,440	442	0.02
Electric lights and fluorescent lamps	—	1,099	—	1,385	771	0.56
Coffee, cocoa, and chocolate preparations	1,446	17,556	12.14	7,117	10,211	1.43
Cement, portland	9,602	6,150	0.64	17,528	2,587	0.15
Wearing apparel	25,041	20,837	0.83	38,618	12,071	0.31
Paper and paper products	758	33,737	44.57	25,846	32,035	1.24
Construction materials	14,689	68,356	4.65	33,800	56,164	1.66
		——1953——			——1956——	
Rubber tires and tubes	—	P23,626	—	P 3,127	P20,742	6.63
Trucks	P12,594	2,546	0.20	30,308	417	0.01
Autos	1,580	3,289	2.08	15,502	2,543	0.15
Steel bars and rods	2,791	6,395	2.29	12,326	3,003	0.24
Ready-mixed paints	2,931	1,863	0.64	16,058	198	0.01
Cotton weaving yarns	2,746	9,493	3.46	7,054	90	0.01
Cotton knitted fabrics	10,277	1,499	0.15	24,093	23	0.00

SOURCE: 1948 and 1954—*Central Bank News Digest*, June 14, 1955; 1953 and 1956—*Central Bank News Digest*, October 15, 1957.

only with explicit permission of the Central Bank), nonessential consumer goods, or nonessential producer goods.

Two other important features of the industrial structure developed in the 1950s: manufacturing production became both increasingly capital-intensive and more dependent on imports of producer goods. The upward trend in the capital-labor ratio is evident from the figures in Table 6-5. Between 1950 and 1959 both the output-capital and output-labor ratios rose. However, the latter ratio increased considerably faster than the former, with the result that

TABLE 6-5

Structural Indices for the Manufacturing Sector of the Philippines, 1950–68
(1955 = 100)

	Ratio: Capital to Labor	Ratio: Output to Capital	Ratio: Output to Labor
1950	61	106	65
1951	76	103	78
1952	87	100	88
1953	96	97	92
1954	99	100	99
1955	100	100	100
1956	97	108	105
1957	92	117	108
1958	103	120	123
1959	106	124	131
1960	118	114	136
1961	121	113	137
1962	118	117	139
1963	124	119	147
1964	127	112	142
1965	126	109	138
1966	132	108	142
1967	139	106	147
1968	142	107	151

SOURCE: George L. Hicks and Geoffrey McNicoll, *Trade and Growth in the Philippines* (Ithaca: Cornell University Press, 1971), p. 68.

Data refer to manufacturing establishments employing five or more persons. Output is measured in value-added terms at constant prices. Capital consists of fixed assets and inventories and is also measured in constant prices.

the capital-labor ratio rose 74 per cent between these years. After 1959 the output-labor ratio continued to rise, though much less rapidly, but the output-capital ratio fell.[2] Thus, both of these changes operated to increase the capital-labor ratio. Since by 1968 the output-capital ratio had declined to its 1950 level, the more than doubling of the capital-labor ratio in manufacturing between these years can be attributed entirely to the increase in the output-labor ratio, i.e., to the failure of employment in manufacturing to rise commensurately with production.

The capital-intensive nature of many of the industries that expanded most rapidly is also apparent from the ratios of capital per worker and capital per unit of value added by industry, shown in Table 6-6. The effect on the average capital-labor ratio in manufacturing of the shifts in industrial composition that were associated with the import-substitution efforts in the early 1950s can be seen if the capital-labor ratios in Table 6-6 are weighted by the value-added shares of these industries in 1938, 1948, 1956, and 1960. The hypothetical average capital-labor ratio for the industries increases from P20,763 in 1938 and P21,867 in 1948 to P27,767 in 1956 and P26,456 in 1960. The 21 per

TABLE 6-6

**Capital, Labor, and Skill Intensities of Philippine
Manufacturing Industries, 1961**

	Capital per Worker (pesos)	Capital per Unit of Value Added	Annual Payroll per Employee[a] (thousands of pesos)
Food, manufactured	17,581	1.909	2.0
Beverages	18,335	1.293	3.1
Tobacco products	11,926	1.400	1.6
Textiles	26,528	6.223	1.7
Footwear and other wearing apparel	6,560	2.866	1.2
Wood products	20,130	5.487	1.7
Furniture and fixtures	12,460	5.326	1.6
Paper and paper products	36,483	4.531	2.6
Printed materials	14,077	2.678	2.7
Leather and leather products	10,740	2.978	1.7
Rubber products	22,231	1.727	2.8
Chemicals	34,381	2.390	3.3
Petroleum products	314,476	1.983	n.a.
Nonmetallic mineral products	34,828	4.379	2.4
Basic metal products	39,385	4.653	2.6
Fabricated metal products	15,663	2.598	2.5
Machinery except electrical	15,880	2.204	2.7
Electrical machinery	27,818	3.756	2.2
Transport equipment	24,118	3.824	2.9
Misc. manufactures	16,268	3.353	2.7
All industries	21,264	2.782	2.1

SOURCE: Capital per worker and capital per value added from Elsa G. Franco, "Capital Intensity of Philippine Manufacturing" (M.A. thesis, University of the Philippines, 1967); annual payroll per worker from Philippine Bureau of Census and Statistics, *Annual Survey of Manufactures, 1960*, Table 1, p. 92.

a. Payroll figures are based on 1960 data.

cent increase between 1948 and 1960 due to the effects of changes in the composition of the industrialization program still accounts for only a small part of the actual percentage increase in the capital-labor ratio in manufacturing between 1950 and 1960. Weighting 1960 annual wages in each industry by the value-added shares of the industries in 1938, 1948, 1956, and 1960 indicates that there was no increase in the average human capital-intensity of production over this period due to shifts in the composition of production. Hypothetical average earnings are P2,020 in 1938, P2,210 in 1948, P2,190 in 1956, and P2,160 in 1960.[3]

The increase in the degree of import dependence of the industrial sector during the 1950s is shown in Table 6-7 by the rise between 1949 and 1960

TABLE 6-7

Imported Industrial Inputs Relative to Industrial Value Added,[a] 1949–64
(1955 prices)

	Ratio to Industrial Value Added of:		
Year	Imported Intermediate Goods	Imported Investment Goods	Imported Intermediate and Investment Goods
1949	.36	.13	.49
1953	.46	.16	.61
1960	.60	.25	.85
1964	.59	.15	.74

SOURCE: D. S. Paauw and J. L. Tryon, "Agriculture-Industry Interrelationships in an Open Dualistic Economy: The Philippines, 1949–1964," in "Growth of Output in the Philippines" (Papers presented at a conference of the International Rice Research Institute, Los Baños, Laguna, December 9–10, 1966; mimeo.).

a. Industrial value added equals the sum of value added in the manufacturing, mining, construction, and transportation sectors.

in the ratios to industrial value added of both imported intermediates and imported investment goods. However, by 1964 the ratio of imported investment goods to value added had declined to its former level, presumably because of the slowdown in the growth of industrial capacity that was associated with the decontrol period.[4]

These resource shifts during the period of exchange control are consistent with those that would be predicted on the basis of knowledge of the protective pattern of the exchange system. The economic subsidies granted on imports of raw materials and capital goods coupled with the protection given to the final output of previously imported, nonessential goods pulled resources into capital-using and import-dependent industries. The use of capital-intensive methods of production was also thereby encouraged in any given industry.

Employment.

In countries with a high rate of population growth, such as the Philippines, an especially important economic goal is to create enough new jobs to match the increase in the labor force. Fortunately, although the labor force growth rate has averaged 3 per cent between 1956 and 1970, employment has increased at the rate of 3.3 per cent.[5] Unemployment, however, has been significant over this entire period. Between 1956 and 1971 it averaged 7.7 per cent of the labor force in May and 6.8 per cent in October and exhibited no clear-cut trend. On an urban-rural breakdown (available only since 1965) the data show a rate of about 9 or 10 per cent in urban areas in contrast to 4 to 7 per cent in rural areas. Needless to say, these figures do not begin to tell the story of the extent of underemployment.[6]

The various trade, monetary, and fiscal policies designed to increase the relative importance of the manufacturing sector have not been the most desirable ones in terms of increasing employment. The elasticity of employment with respect to value added in manufacturing is the lowest of all the productive sectors. For example, studies by Mangahas, Meyers, and Barker and by Oshima place this elasticity at 0.5 in manufacturing in contrast to 2.5 for mining, 1.2 for transportation, 1.3 for commerce, 1.1 for services, 0.7 for agriculture, and 1.0 for construction.[7] The comparatively low employment-creating nature of the industrialization process can also be brought out by noting that, although the real stock of capital utilized in manufacturing increased 428 per cent and real output in manufacturing rose 430 per cent between 1950 and 1968, employment in this sector increased only 128 per cent.[8]

Exports.

As industrial production in the Philippines has become highly import-dependent, the ability to earn foreign exchange through exporting has become increasingly important for continued growth of the economy. The average annual increase in the volume of exports over the entire 1950–70 period was 5.5 per cent. This can be demarcated into an annual rate of 5.9 per cent from 1950 to 1960 and 5.0 per cent between 1960 and 1970.

Although the Philippines is usually thought of as an exporter of primary products, actually six of the ten leading exports as of 1969 were classified as manufactured products in the Census of Manufactures, namely, sugar, coconut oil, desiccated coconut, canned pineapples, veneer, and plywood. These six accounted for 36 per cent of total exports in 1949 and 32 per cent in 1970 (see Table 1-3). The other four major export products, accounting for about 50 per cent of the value of exports in both 1949 and 1950, are copra (dried coconut meal from which coconut oil is extracted), abaca (the source of Manila hemp), logs and lumber, and copper concentrates. Although the total export contribution of these four primary products has remained roughly the same between 1949 and 1970, there has been a sharp shift within the group. The two agricultural goods, copra and abaca, constituted 48 per cent of total export value in 1949, whereas logs and lumber and copper concentrates amounted to only 2 per cent. By 1970 copra and abaca had dropped to 9 per cent, and logs and lumber and copper concentrates had risen to 41 per cent. Minor exports accounted for 24 per cent of all exports in 1949 and 17 per cent in 1970.

Exports of sugar have been almost entirely a function of the U.S. quota because the United States has been an extremely profitable market for foreign producers. Except for a few short periods, the U.S. price has always been above the world price in postwar years. In early 1970, for example, the U.S. price for raw sugar was 6.88 cents per pound, whereas the world price was only 3.27 cents per pound. A quota of 980,000 short tons (raw value) was first granted to the Philippines in 1934.[9] (Producers in the Virgin Islands, Cuba, and Puerto Rico, as well as the United States also were allocated quotas.) This was not changed until 1960, when the quota was increased by 70,000 short tons. Shortly thereafter, an embargo was placed on Cuban sugar, and additional imports from other foreign producers were permitted. Between 1960 and 1962 the Philippines was able to sell to the United States almost 800,000 tons more than its regular quota. Although the supplementary allocations due to the Cuban embargo were gradually reduced, a further 76,000 short tons of sugar imports were allowed each year under the Sugar Act of 1965, bringing the quota to 1,126,000 tons. Subsequently, 47 per cent of any short-fall in the quota exports of Puerto Rico and the Virgin Islands was added to the Philippine import quota. Except for the drought year of 1957 as well as in 1961 and 1963, the U.S. quota has in effect been filled since 1954, when the industry first regained its prewar capacity.

The other major food export of the Philippines, namely, coconut products (mainly in the form of copra, desiccated coconut, copra meal, and coconut oil) has declined significantly in relative importance since the early 1950s. In 1950, for example, the export value of these four products amounted to 54 per cent of the value of all exports; by 1970 this had fallen to 20 per cent.

However, despite this decline in coconut products as a whole, the export share of coconut oil actually rose from about 4 per cent in 1950 to 9 per cent in 1970. A major reason for this seems to have been the fall in ocean freight rates for coconut oil due to the introduction of bulk tankers.[10] The export share attributable to copra meal or cake also increased slightly.

The coconut oil and desiccated coconut industries have been helped by tax preferences in the U.S. market. A study of the effect of preferential treatment on the Philippine economy between 1900 and 1940 indicates that the degree of processing in the coconut industry as well as in the sugar and abaca industries was increased significantly as a result of the preferences granted by the United States.[11] Until 1974, the duty on imports of Philippine coconut oil into the United States was only 1 cent per pound, whereas the duty on imports from other foreign producers was 3 or 4 cents, depending upon whether or not they were members of GATT.[12] Similarly, imports of desiccated coconut from the Philippines are subject to only 60 per cent of the tariff of 1.75 cents per pound. In 1974, when U.S.-Philippine preferential arrangements ended, coconut oil from the Philippines became subject to the full duty of 4 cents per pound; and desiccated coconut, to the full duty of 1.75 cents per pound. The general view seems to be that the elimination of preferential treatment will not significantly affect these two industries,[13] although the responsiveness of output to price changes that are reported below casts some doubt on this prediction.

Bautista and Encarnación, in a study of export supply equations, have found that relative prices play a significant role in coconut oil exports as well as exports of copra and desiccated coconut. Specifically, their export supply equation for copra is:[14]

$$X_{cp} = -541.2 + 1.933\,P_{cp} - 1.755\,P_{dc} + .8421\;Y_{cp}$$
$$\phantom{X_{cp} = -541.2 + }(2.11)\quad (-2.42)\qquad (5.83)$$

$R^2 = .939$; Durbin-Watson statistic $(D.W.) = 2.40$; years covered, 1962–68

where X_{cp} = exports of copra (in thousands of metric tons); P_{cp} = export price index of copra (1955 = 100); P_{dc} = export price index of desiccated coconut (1955 = 100); and Y_{cp} = domestic output of coconuts (expressed in units of copra) in thousands of metric tons. The own-price elasticity of export supply for copra is 0.49 at the mean values, while the cross-elasticity for desiccated coconut is -0.42. These estimates are used as part of a larger model to project Philippine exports to 1976.[15] The increase in the price of copra is assumed to be 3 per cent; in the price of dessicated coconut, 5 per cent; and in the output of coconuts, 3.31 per cent. On that basis, the export supply of copra is expected to rise at an annual rate of 4.7 per cent between 1972 and 1976.

For coconut oil exports, the best equation estimated by these authors is:

$$X_{co} = -1,393.8 + .8670\, P_{co} + 60.365\, \frac{W_n}{P_n} + .4126\, Y_{cp}$$
$$\qquad\qquad\quad (3.68) \qquad\quad (3.42) \qquad\quad (4.61)$$

$$R^2 = .822; \ D.W. = 2.17; \text{ years covered, 1962–68}$$

where X_{co} = exports of coconut oil (in thousands of metric tons); P_{co} = export price index of coconut oil (1955 = 100); W_n = annual money wage rate in manufacturing (in pesos); P_n = implicit price index for manufacturing value added (1955 = 100); Y_{cp} = domestic output of coconuts expressed in equivalent units of copra (in thousands of metric tons). The W_n/P_n term is inserted to reflect the point that the higher the real wages in manufacturing, the lower will be the derived local demand for use in manufacturing of such products as margarine, cooking oil, and soap. This, in turn, means that exports will be higher. The export supply elasticity of coconut oil at the mean values is 0.80. Bautista and Encarnación estimate that exports of coconut oil will grow at an average annual rate of 10 per cent between 1972 and 1976.[16]

In the case of desiccated coconut, which is almost entirely exported, Bautista and Encarnación postulate that export supply is a function of the size of the capital stock and the labor force employed in the industry. The size of the capital stock, in turn, depends upon past prices of desiccated coconut and copra, since these affect the profitability of investment. Again, these price terms are significant in the authors' estimates of the export supply function. The expected average annual increase in the quantity of desiccated coconut between 1972 and 1976 is 6.0 per cent.

Another agricultural product that has declined rapidly in relative importance as an export is abaca. Synthetic fibers have made heavy inroads into the market for Manila hemp, and between 1949 and 1970 the export share of abaca fell from about 12 per cent of total exports to about 1.5 per cent. By 1976 the Encarnación group estimates that abaca exports will disappear.

Since the mid-1960s, the largest contributor to the foreign-exchange earnings of the Philippines has been logs and lumber. In 1970 the export share of logs and lumber was 23.5 per cent and, if veneer and plywood are added to the figure, the total rises to nearly 27 per cent. The export supply equation estimated by Bautista and Encarnación for logs and lumber is as follows:

$$X_{ll} = -861.2 + 16.178\, P_{ll} - 7.030\, P_{pl} + .327\, Y_l$$
$$\qquad\qquad (4.05) \qquad (-2.55) \qquad (1.99)$$

$$R^2 = .877; \ s = 429.4; \ D.W. = .321; \text{ years covered, 1950–69}$$

where X_{ll} = supply of logs and lumber (in millions of board feet); P_{ll} and P_{pl} = export price indices (1955 = 100) for logs and lumber and for plywood, respectively; and Y_l = domestic output of logs in millions of board feet. The own-price elasticity of export supply is 1.33 at the mean values, and the cross-price elasticity is -0.405. The authors found that exports of plywood depended solely on the domestic output of plywood. This, in turn, depended upon past levels of production and past levels of the export price of plywood relative to logs.

There is considerable concern in the Philippines about the ability of log exports to continue to serve as the main source of Philippine export growth. In addition to the depletion effects of the rapid growth of authorized logging, commercial forest areas have been reduced at an alarming rate in recent years by illegal logging, land clearing, and shifting cultivation.[17] A forestry expert from the United Nations Food and Agricultural Organization has estimated that the average annual growth rate of logs and lumber exports during the decade from 1975 to 1985 will drop from its 10.7 per cent average between 1960 and 1970 to, at best, a growth rate of 1 per cent and, at worst, to an annual decline of 15 per cent.[18] However, the Encarnación group projects an annual average growth rate of 4.4 per cent for logs and lumber between 1972 and 1976. The wood and lumber industry in the Philippines also is not as pessimistic as the UN expert. A trade association representing the industry expects log exports to level off during the 1970s but exports of processed wood products to increase. The association's projection is that export earnings for all wood products will rise about 2.5 per cent annually from 1972 to 1980.[19]

Exports of copper concentrates have also grown very rapidly since 1949. Since this output is entirely exported, the export supply equations fitted by Bautista and Encarnación were similar to those used for desiccated coconut and abaca. The best equation is:

$$X_{cc} = -912.4 + .7245\ SP_{cc} - .1138\ SW_q + 156.7\ t$$
$$(2.46) \qquad (-2.36) \qquad (2.66)$$

$$R^2 = .934;\ D.W. = 2.90;\ \text{years covered, } 1956\text{-}68$$

where X_{cc} = export supply (in thousands of metric tons); SP_{cc} = sum of export price index of copper concentrates from t (time period) = 0 to $t - 1$;[20] SW_q = sum of annual money wage rates in mining from $t = 0$ to $t - 1$; and t is a time variable running from 0 in 1956 to 12 in 1968. Copper exports are expected by the Encarnación group to decline at an average annual rate of 3.3 per cent between 1972 and 1976.

The export supply of so-called minor exports, i.e., those not included in the list of the ten principal exports, could best be explained by Bautista and Encarnación on the basis of an equation which includes total exports lagged one year (an expectations proxy) and the exchange rate. According to this equation, an increase in the exchange rate between the dollar and peso by 1 peso increases exports of these commodities by P42.3 million.

The various equations fitted by Bautista and Encarnación clearly establish that the supply of Philippine exports is sensitive to the peso price of these exports and thus, through the relations between these prices and the exchange rate, to exchange-rate policy.[21] A very rough estimate can be made of the magnitude of the increase in the value of exports that would have been possible with a peso that was less overvalued. Suppose that in the period 1950 through 1969, the effective exchange rate applicable to exports was not the actual export rate but either the rate applicable to essential producer goods or that applicable to semiessential consumer goods. An equilibrium rate probably was somewhere between these two rates. Also assume for simplicity—although this is clearly not the case for copra and coconut oil—that the demand for Philippine exports in dollars is perfectly elastic. In this case, export prices in pesos will change in the same proportion as changes in the exchange rate. With these assumptions it is possible to estimate from the supply equations of Bautista and Encarnación the amount by which the average annual level of export earnings in the 1950–69 period under these hypothetical exchange rates exceeds the actual average annual level of export earnings in the same period. Because of the dependence of sugar exports on the size of the U.S. quota, the two authors did not estimate an export supply function for this commodity. Therefore, it is assumed that exports of sugar would have remained unchanged. It also turns out that applying the supply elasticities implied by the estimates of Bautista and Encarnación for desiccated coconut to the entire 1950–70 period yields negative values for the change in the export earnings for this product, because of cross-elasticity effects. Clearly, it would be erroneous to conclude that raising the price of all coconut products by the same proportion would actually decrease the dollar value of the exports of this commodity. However, it will be assumed that the supply elasticity of this product with respect to changes in peso prices is zero. Thus, dollar earnings from exports of desiccated coconut are assumed to remain unchanged at the new hypothetical exchange rates.

With the effective exchange rate applicable to essential producer goods, the average annual dollar level of exports from 1950 through 1969 would have exceeded the actual average annual export level during this period by $116 million. This increase is composed of the following commodity changes (in millions of dollars): sugar products, $0; copra, $13.0; coconut oil, $8.2; desiccated coconut, $0; abaca, $21.9; logs and lumber, $39.2; copper concentrates, $22.1; and minor exports, $11.4.[22] The $116 million figure represents a 20 per cent increase over the actual average annual value of commodity exports from 1950 to 1969. Alternatively, it may be assumed that peso prices increase in proportion to the excess of the effective exchange rate for semi-essential consumer goods over the effective exchange rate for exports. On that basis, the average annual level of exports increases from 1950 to 1969 by $188 million. The increase breaks down as follows (in millions of dollars): sugar products, $0; copra, $19.8; coconut oil, $12.2; desiccated coconut, $0; abaca, $32.8; logs and lumber, $59.0; copper concentrates, $33.2; and minor exports, $31.5. This hypothetical export level is 33 per cent above the average annual export level from 1950 to 1969. While these estimates must be taken only as very rough approximations, they do add support to what has been directly observed about exchange rate changes, namely, that the value of exports is quite responsive to currency depreciations. However, in both cases, about one-third of the increase in export earnings is due to greater exports of logs and lumber. In view of the existing depletion of the country's forests, it might be argued either that the export supply equation used would no longer apply if attempts were made to expand log and lumber exports significantly or that, even if it did, the government should not permit such an increase. Nevertheless, the rise in export earnings under the two hypothetical exchange rates is still substantial without projecting any increase at all in the logs and lumber sector.

Not only has export growth been retarded by effective exchange rates that discriminated against the export sector, but export expansion has been hampered by the import-substitution program, since this has artificially inflated the prices of some inputs used by the export sector. Examples where the rise in input prices resulted in negative rates of effective protection in the export sector were given in the last chapter. A rough estimate of the cost of discouraging the production of processed wood products such as veneer and plywood by means of discriminatory trade policies has been made by Gerardo P. Sicat.[23] One of his estimates is based on the assumption that the volume of logs and lumber exported was only one-half of the actual amount but that these timber products were first processed into other wood products, for example, plywood, before being exported. He found that under this assumption the annual increase in domestic value added would have been about one-third of 1 per cent of gross national product prior to 1962 and 1 per cent of GNP thereafter. Not only would this be a significant gain, but it would permit the timber resources of the Philippines to be depleted at a much less rapid rate.

Since the Philippines now wishes to promote selective programs both of import substitution and export expansion, it must find ways of eliminating the costs of the former program from the latter. One possible but fairly crude method of achieving this would be to use input-output data to estimate the increases in input costs caused by protection for a particular product and then to pay exporters this sum for each unit of the product they export. This solution would, of course, require assurance by importing countries against retaliatory action on grounds of export subsidization by the Philippines.

GROWTH EFFECTS

There seems no doubt that the Philippine exchange-control system played a significant part in the industrialization activities of the country during the early 1950s. As pointed out in Chapter 2, the emergence of exchange controls as a significant allocating device was related generally to the immediate postwar consumption boom, but more specifically to the election year exchange crisis of 1949. By greatly restricting imports of nonessential consumption goods and nonessential producer goods while adopting a liberal import policy with respect to intermediate inputs and capital goods, the government's actions led to high profit rates in many import-competing manufacturing lines and, as pointed out in the first section of this chapter, thereby brought about a major shift of resources into the manufacturing sector. Various other fiscal and monetary policies reinforced this pattern of development, but the scarcity-creating effects of restricting imports of so-called nonessential manufactures through exchange controls was the major means of promoting industrialization.

From the beginning of the exchange control period, in 1950, until 1956, growth in the manufacturing sector proceeded at an average annual rate of 13.5 per cent, whereas the rate in the agricultural sector was about 6.4 per cent. Real net domestic product rose an average of 8.0 per cent per year. By most standards, all these growth rates would be judged to be highly satisfactory. Moreover, they were achieved with a ratio of gross domestic capital formation to GNP that averaged only about 13 per cent. After 1956, however, growth rates in the Philippine economy slackened, especially in the manufacturing sector. The real growth rate in this sector dropped to an annual average of 6.3 per cent from 1957 to 1960 and to only 4.0 per cent from 1961 to 1965. Net domestic product rose at an average annual rate of 4.6 per cent from 1957 to 1960 and at a rate of 5.0 per cent from 1961 to 1965. From 1966 to 1969, growth rates accelerated somewhat, to 5.2 per cent for manufacturing and 5.6 per cent for net domestic product. In 1970, manufacturing growth fell to only 2.0 per cent but increased to 7.4 per cent in 1971. Net domestic product increased at rates of 4.5 per cent and 3.3 per cent, respectively, in 1970 and 1971.

As many countries have discovered, during the early period of an import-substitution program it is relatively easy to maintain a high growth rate in the manufacturing sector by diverting consumer demands for simple manufactures from foreign to domestic producers. But it becomes increasingly difficult to maintain growth rates in this sector above those in the rest of the economy as the ability to capture established market demands narrows and local manufacturers are forced to enter product lines that are technologically more complex or are more capital-intensive. Since import-substituting production relies heavily on imports of raw materials and capital goods, the growth rate may also be constrained by a shortage of foreign exchange.

The narrowing of import-substitution opportunities for simple consumer goods appears to have been the most important factor in accounting for the slowdown in manufacturing growth after the mid-1950s. As is indicated in Table 6-8, the extent to which consumption demand was diverted from the

TABLE 6-8

Percentage Distribution of Imports, 1949–69

	1949	1951–53	1955–57	1959–61	1963–65	1967–69[a]
Producer goods	62.7	76.8	81.7	86.1	83.9	87.9
Machinery and equipment	9.9	9.1	11.0	19.7	17.4	19.9
Unprocessed raw materials	1.0	1.6	4.2	10.4	15.4	13.1
Semiprocessed raw materials	41.6	48.0	51.3	45.8	45.9	50.2
Supplies	10.1	18.0	15.2	10.2	5.1	4.5
Consumer goods	37.3	23.2	18.3	13.9	16.4	12.1
Durable	2.5	1.6	1.3	0.8	1.0	1.1
Nondurable	34.8	21.6	17.0	13.1	15.4	11.1

SOURCE: John H. Power and Gerardo P. Sicat, *The Philippines: Industrialization and Trade Policies* (London: Oxford University Press, 1971), p. 39.
a. First half of 1969 only.

foreign sector to domestic producers was very impressive in the early 1950s. The share of consumption goods in imports was reduced from 37 per cent in 1949 to 18 per cent for 1955–57. The capital goods share rose somewhat between these years, but the greatest increase occurred in the intermediate goods sector. As was already pointed out in the discussion of Table 6-3, the extent of import substitution in these early years was very significant in many industries.

The government had no wish to limit industrialization to the easily captured markets for very simply processed manufactures. It continued to tighten controls over the importation of those consumer and producer goods that seemed capable of being produced at not "unreasonable" costs within the Philippines. By 1959, nonessential consumer goods constituted only 1.1 per cent of total imports, and nonessential producer goods, only 3.7 per cent (see Table 2-6), while essential producer goods reached 61.3 per cent.

One of the most interesting aspects of Philippine growth, which first becomes noticeable during the mid-1950s and continues until the mid-1960s (see Table 1-5), is the gradual increase in the ratio of gross domestic capital formation to gross national product. This was not due to a relative increase in the inflow of foreign funds, but rather to a sharp increase in personal and corporate savings (especially the former). In 1953–54 these two categories of savings constituted 80 per cent of total net savings (general government and net borrowing from abroad making up the rest), whereas in 1958–59 they amounted to 91 per cent of net savings. It is tempting to argue that the import-substitution program helped to increase domestic savings by creating very attractive profit opportunities in manufacturing, thereby encouraging own-savings. Sicat and Hooley, in a study of investment demand for 200 firms, found, for example, that profits were by far the major determinant of gross investment.[24] They also concluded that investment in manufacturing displayed a strong profits-push type of behavior rather than a sales pull.[25] However, since the investment ratio continued to rise during and after the liberalization period and there was no significant change in the rate of this increase, it does not seem possible to say that the exchange-control system (or the liberalization program) had any significant effect on the investment ratio. A detailed study of savings patterns in the country is very much needed; perhaps after that is made, some relationship between the nature of the exchange-control regime and savings propensities may be found.

The rise in the ratio of gross domestic capital formation to GNP implies that given increments in the capital stock of the Philippines resulted in successively smaller increments in output, i.e., the incremental capital-output ratio increased. This trend can be observed from the behavior of the ratio of the annual volume of gross domestic capital formation to the yearly change in gross domestic product (GDP). The average yearly level of this ratio during various subperiods from 1946 to 1971 is as follows: 1946–50, 1.03; 1951–55, 1.62; 1956–60, 3.08; 1961–65, 3.67; 1966–71, 3.8.[26] The rise in this figure after 1955 is especially remarkable and confirms that the system of incentives established by the government increasingly shifted production into highly capital-using forms after that date. The upward trend also occurred in the manufacturing sector. In this sector the ratio of the change in the real value of fixed assets to the change in real value added is as follows: 1958, 0.55; 1960, 0.63; 1962, 0.99; 1964, 0.99; 1966 and 1968 (average), 0.85.[27]

An important complement to the increased savings response has been the emergence of an active entrepreneurial group within the Philippines. As has been documented by others,[28] a vigorous and economically bold group quickly moved into manufacturing from such activities as commerce, finance, and traditional exports. Thus, in terms of helping to create an entrepreneurial group, the industrialization program was successful, even though this accomplishment might have been achieved at lower resource costs.

As noted in discussions of several economic variables, e.g., growth rates and incremental capital-output ratios, the nature of post-World War II economic growth in the Philippines prior to around 1955 or 1956 seems quite different than after these years. In a study of the sources of economic growth between 1947 and 1965, Jeffrey Williamson analyzes this difference in some detail.[29] For the 1947–55 period he finds that the sources of the average annual aggregate growth rate of 7.3 per cent can be attributed to the following factors: increase in the labor force, 1.93 per cent; increase in the stock of land, 0.30 per cent; increase in the capital stock, 0.99 per cent; and technical improvements, 4.08 per cent.[30] The average annual growth rate for 1955–65 was only 4.5 per cent and can be broken down as follows: labor, 1.93 per cent; land, 0.36 per cent; capital, 1.68 per cent; and technical change, 0.53 per cent. The sharp increase in the relative importance of the growth contribution of capital in the second period and the significant decline in the contribution made by technical change underscore the basic differences in the nature of growth prior to and after the mid-1950s.

Williamson suggests that the high contribution of technological improvements in the first period is related to the fact that this period is one of revival following wartime destruction.[31] He notes, however, that in the 1955–65 period increases in the productivity of traditional inputs were unimpressive not only in comparison with the earlier period, but also in comparison with such countries as Taiwan or Japan. The analysis here seems to indicate that the rapid growth rate for 1947–55 also was partly due to an initially successful import-substitution program that diverted purchases of simple manufactured goods from abroad to the domestic sector. After the mid-1950s it became much more difficult to raise growth rates by import substitution. However, the pattern of protection and subsidization still made investment in capital-intensive industries and the use of capital-intensive methods in general appear to be potentially profitable. Thus, the rate of growth in the capital stock increased, even though the over-all growth rate declined.

Another aspect of the difference in the nature of growth after the mid-1950s is the creation of excess capacity in manufacturing. Unfortunately, no comprehensive time series on the degree of capacity utilization exists, but the fact that there was little discussion of the problem during the first part of the 1950s suggests that excess capacity did not become a significant problem until the last part of the decade. In a 1959 questionnaire sent out by the American Chamber of Commerce of the Philippines, 28 of the 50 responding manufacturing firms stated that they were operating below capacity.[32] The median level of capacity utilization was 50 per cent. That the problem still existed in 1970 is indicated in Table 6-9, where capacity utilization rates are listed for industries officially declared to be overcrowded.

TABLE 6-9

List of Industries with Excess Capacity, 1970

Industry	Capacity Utiliza- tion	Industry	Capacity Utiliza- tion
Meat processing	20%	Flour milling	45%
Beer brewing	80	Soft drinks	35
Alcoholic drinks	77	Air conditioners	26
Refrigerators	65	Automotive assembly	17
Sewing machines	15	Electric and gas stoves	24
Radios and phonographs	30	Cement	80
Soaps and detergents	77	Storage batteries	55
Pipes	18	Ammonium sulphate	25
Complex and mixed fertilizers	44	Superphosphate	5
Nails	25	Nonintegrated paper plants	75
Cold rolling steel mills	32	Tin plating	35
Leather tanning	n.a.	Truck assembly	16
Wheeled tractor assembly	28	Cordage	n.a.
Steel wires	28	Rubber tires	81
Bar mills	10	Light bulbs	22
Copper wires	22	Sugar processing	87
Paints, varnishes, and allied products	52		

n.a. = not available.

SOURCE: UN Economic Commission for Asia and the Far East, "Country Study on the Philippines" (Paper presented at Asian Conference on Industrialization, Tokyo, Japan, September 8–21, 1970; mimeo.).

Under current government policy, expansion in such industries will not receive tax exemption privileges. In the 1950s and 1960s, however, no such attempt to control excess capacity was made. In some instances in those years, markets for particular differentiated products were probably not large enough to utilize fully an optimum-sized plant. Yet the degree of output protection and subsidization of inputs was sufficiently high to make production profitable at low levels of capacity utilization. In a number of cases, producers were encouraged to expand capacity because of the favorable exchange rate and liberal exchange allocations for capital goods but were then unable to obtain the necessary foreign exchange with which to purchase imported intermediate inputs once the additional capacity was installed.[33] In other cases, the entry of new firms into an industry may have led to a market-sharing, monopolistic solution in which capacity utilization rates were reduced but prices were kept high enough for most firms to maintain comfortable profit levels. The controls on the supply of foreign exchange for any industry in themselves acted to prevent entry of enough new firms to eliminate monopolistic price and output policies.

In addition to the constraints imposed by the size of domestic markets, another factor that increasingly acted to limit the Philippine growth rate after the liberalization episode was the low growth rate of export earnings. During the first part of the 1950s insufficient foreign exchange with which to purchase producer goods from abroad was not a significant problem. The sharp rise in exports at the time of the Korean War boom, in 1950–51, the considerable room that then existed for cutting back on nonessential consumption goods, the large reserves built up with U.S. aid, and the comparatively low import-requiring nature of the early industrialization all prevented this. In the last half of the 1950s the problem was still not serious, largely because the value of exports rose at an average annual rate of about 10 per cent, due in part to an increase in export prices. An expansion of foreign borrowing also helped prevent a foreign-exchange problem.

Even though nonagricultural production had become highly import-dependent by the early 1960s, severe pressures on the supplies of foreign exchange needed for intermediate and investment goods still continued to be offset in the first part of the 1960s by the favorable effects of the decontrol program on exports. However, with the expansion of manufacturing and infrastructure activities after this period and the consequent growing overvaluation of the Philippine peso, the constraint imposed on growth by the need to import producer goods became more and more obvious. The significant rise in imports that was associated with economic growth after 1966 was not financed by growing exports, but instead by short-term foreign borrowing. When sources of this type of borrowing became exhausted and exports continued to stagnate, the foreign-exchange crisis of 1969–70 brought about a dramatic end to the expansionary phase and again forced a devaluation in order to generate additional foreign exchange.

DISTRIBUTIONAL EFFECTS

A useful way of gaining insights into the pattern of economic development in countries such as the Philippines is to analyze the economic interrelationships between the agricultural and industrial sectors during the growth process.[34] The focus of this analysis is on the manner by which the agricultural surplus required both to feed a growing labor force in the industrial sector and to purchase additional producer goods from abroad is made available to the industrial sector in exchange for manufactured goods, and then how this two-way exchange behaves over time in response to various development policies and such basic factors as population growth and technical progress.

The Philippines is fortunate in possessing an agricultural sector that has long been capable of producing a sizable surplus over and above the basic needs of the rural population. This rural population is divided into two main groups: (1) those who grow food crops (principally rice and corn) for domestic consumption and have a surplus above their own needs and (2) those who produce traditional export commodities. Prior to the deliberate industrialization efforts of the postwar period, foreign exchange earned by the latter group provided the economy with its machinery and equipment needs and certain essential intermediate products such as mineral fuels and lubricants plus a wide variety of manufactured consumption goods, many of which would be considered nonessential in terms of basic needs. However, the agricultural surplus was not entirely used in importing manufactured goods. A portion was used not only to provide the urban services needed to undertake export and import activities but also to purchase some domestically manufactured goods. Before World War II these local manufacturing activities, which had developed as a result of agricultural growth, mainly involved processing food, making cigarettes and cigars, and distilling or blending liquor.[35]

In the early 1950s the government effectively rechanneled a significant part of the agricultural surplus by introducing exchange controls and greatly limiting imports of so-called nonessential goods. This turned the market demand for these products inward and imposed greater demands on the uses of the surplus for importing capital goods and intermediate production inputs.

There are several potential obstacles to continued growth under these import-substituting conditions. One of the most important of these is a failure of the agricultural surplus to grow at a rate sufficient to sustain the high import requirements of the industrialization process. Producers of traditional export commodities tend to decrease their output levels because of the adverse income effects brought about by the higher prices for manufactured goods as well as the increasing extent of currency overvaluation that is used to subsidize the industrialization process. As already pointed out, a failure of this sort halted the growth efforts of the Marcos administration from 1966 to 1969. The government shaped a development strategy that not only imposed import demands far above reasonable expectations of export earnings, but also produced repercussions which halted the growth of the surplus.

A second form in which a decline of the agricultural surplus may take place is through a shortage of basic domestic foodstuffs that causes food prices to rise. During the period of vigorous Philippine industrialization efforts in the 1950s, this does not seem to have been a problem. In part, food prices did not rise significantly because, at least until recently, the country had some of the features of a land-surplus economy.[36] During the 1950s, adequate new land and technical knowledge were available for the growing rural population to expand food production sufficiently to prevent any major pressures on food prices. The wholesale price index for domestically produced agricultural goods for home consumption (1955 = 100) was 111 in 1950 and 110 in 1960. However, the government also used a part of the surplus for importing basic foodstuffs, especially rice, in order to assure adequate food supplies for the industrialization efforts. Actually, as previously noted, the period in which rising food prices threatened the industrialization process through a rise in money wages and a cut in manufacturers' profits was during the decontrol period in the early 1960s.

In terms of the effects of relative price changes in products sold versus products bought, the agricultural sector was penalized during the early period of industrialization, as is indicated in Table 6-10. Between the periods 1949–52 and 1956–59, average prices of agricultural products for home consumption fell by 9 per cent, and average export prices of agricultural goods fell by nearly 6 per cent. On the other hand, between these same periods, domestic prices of imported goods rose nearly 10 per cent, and prices of domestically produced nonagricultural goods remained unchanged.

The liberalization episode from 1960 to 1965 brought a marked improvement in the terms of trade to agricultural producers. Between 1960 and 1965, prices of agricultural goods for home consumption rose 38 per cent; those for exports rose 52 per cent. At the same time, prices of imported goods rose only 24 per cent, and nonagricultural domestic goods, only 18 per cent. The terms of trade continued to improve somewhat between 1966 and 1969 as the government's borrowing policy proved able to hold down the prices of imports. The 1970 devaluation temporarily worsened the trading terms for agricultural producers of domestically consumed items, but by 1971 they had essentially regained their 1969 relative position. Traditional exporters, however, gained moderately as a result of the peso depreciation.

As a consequence of the country's ability throughout most of the industrialization episode to provide foodstuffs to feed the expanding urban population without encountering significant increasing real costs in agriculture, it has been possible to attract labor to the cities without bidding up real wages. Indeed, one of the remarkable facts about the postwar development period is that real wages have not improved for the industrial labor force. The behavior of employment and of money and real wages of industrial workers together by sector is shown in Table 6-11. During the phase of rapid growth between

TABLE 6-10

**Import Prices and Prices of Domestic Products for
Home Consumption and for Export,[a] 1949–71**
(1955 = 100)

	Domestic Prices of Imported Goods	Prices of Domestic Goods for Home Consumption		Prices of Domestic Goods for Export	
		Agricultural	Nonagricultural	Agricultural	Nonagricultural
1949	84.4	123.5	106.8	124.2	100.2
1950	102.5	111.2	99.7	141.2	104.8
1951	128.9	122.2	109.4	147.0	106.7
1952	114.4	111.2	106.1	100.0	101.6
1953	108.5	106.3	107.3	133.8	113.5
1954	105.2	100.2	102.8	110.9	106.2
1955	100.0	100.0	100.0	100.0	100.0
1956	108.8	101.7	102.3	104.6	102.8
1957	114.6	107.9	104.3	111.6	98.1
1958	119.2	111.2	105.9	125.0	104.0
1959	129.9	103.5	109.9	141.7	115.2
1960	137.4	110.1	112.7	138.4	111.7
1961	144.5	117.8	117.0	145.1	110.1
1962	158.2	117.6	121.5	178.5	121.8
1963	167.8	133.4	126.9	217.6	129.8
1964	169.4	148.0	130.4	208.8	133.1
1965	170.2	152.0	133.6	210.7	155.4
1966	172.3	165.8	136.6	208.6	154.8
1967	173.5	176.6	140.0	231.6	155.1
1968	174.6	179.6	142.6	262.0	167.3
1969	178.2	181.6	144.9	249.8	166.1
1970	220.9	207.2	173.6	330.0	204.7
1971	245.3	239.5	184.3	364.2	198.4

SOURCE: Central Bank of the Philippines.
a. All indices are for wholesale prices.

1949 and 1956 labor held its own or, as in the case of unskilled workers, improved its real wage position somewhat. The inflation of 1950–51 reduced real wages sharply, but the government at this time was much concerned about the real-income position of lower-income groups. Consequently, special efforts were made to keep the prices of "essentials" from rising in 1950–51,

TABLE 6-11

Wages and Employment in the Nonagricultural Sector, 1949-71
(1955 = 100)

	Money Wages		Real Wages		Employment				
	Skilled	Un-skilled	Skilled	Un-skilled	Mfr.	Constr.	Com-merce	Transp. & Comm.	Govt.
1949	102.3	94.6	100.7	93.1	86.2	251.1	97.9	101.4	76.3
1950	102.2	82.8	97.6	79.1	84.4	175.1	91.5	99.6	78.4
1951	95.8	89.4	84.5	78.8	85.3	110.3	88.6	94.9	82.8
1952	97.4	95.6	91.8	90.1	85.4	127.9	93.1	98.0	87.7
1953	99.5	98.3	97.1	95.9	94.0	116.8	91.7	99.6	92.0
1954	100.0	97.1	99.0	96.1	99.6	138.9	95.1	100.1	92.0
1955	100.0	100.0	100.0	100.0	100.0	100.0	100.0	100.0	100.0
1956	100.3	101.5	97.7	98.8	100.5	114.9	106.8	106.5	111.4
1957	100.0	100.4	95.7	96.1	106.2	135.8	119.1	112.1	117.8
1958	103.5	101.0	95.8	93.5	106.5	151.1	122.3	116.2	121.8
1959	105.3	101.8	98.4	95.1	111.6	157.5	121.2	115.5	130.7
1960	105.1	101.9	94.3	91.4	115.3	167.4	119.7	123.4	133.0
1961	104.8	104.4	92.6	92.2	117.0	177.3	119.8	135.0	138.3
1962	106.1	107.5	88.6	89.7	118.8	161.2	125.8	143.8	145.0
1963	109.3	113.4	86.4	89.6	121.3	161.5	131.1	143.4	152.8
1964	111.2	114.4	81.2	83.6	123.3	165.2	135.9	143.5	160.3
1965	114.4	122.5	81.5	87.3	127.0	173.7	145.0	141.2	164.3
1966	120.1	131.4	80.6	88.2	125.6	191.4	141.3	139.6	163.3
1967	125.7	137.6	79.8	87.3	127.2	185.3	137.9	141.5	164.4
1968	135.8	153.1	86.0	96.9	130.6	199.9	141.8	146.6	166.6
1969	143.0	160.3	89.2	100.0	132.5	193.3	140.8	149.7	170.7
1970	151.9	177.9	80.9	94.5	132.4	191.8	140.1	157.8	172.1
1971	159.9	189.9	71.5	85.1	132.6	193.5	142.6	161.1	174.5

SOURCE: Central Bank of the Philippines, *Statistical Bulletin*, December 1971.

and liberal foreign-exchange allotments were continued for this category of commodities after the Korean War period. However, in the last half of the decade, real wages fell, as they continued to do throughout the decontrol period. Near the end of the 1960s, when the country engaged in the experience of living beyond its means, real wages began to rise, but this upward movement was sharply reversed with the currency depreciation of 1970.

It should not be concluded from the absence of an increase in real wages that labor has not benefited at all from the country's industrialization. Real wages in industry have remained about twice[37] as high as in agriculture throughout the entire period, and the transference of labor from agriculture to industry has thus resulted in an increase in labor's absolute income share. The share of the labor force employed in agriculture declined from 72 per cent in 1952 to 57 per cent by 1967.[38] Furthermore, within the urban labor force many have benefited from the relatively greater use of skilled and technical labor as manufacturing and tertiary services (especially government services) have expanded.

The major beneficiaries of the government's development policies have been those who own or control businesses in the industrial sector. Exchange-control as well as related import-substitution policies created enormous windfall gains and profit opportunities in the industrial sector, which were then exploited by a vigorous Philippine entrepreneurial group. In response to the incentives devised by the government, a large share of these profits was, of course, plowed back into the economy in the form of additional capital, much of which unfortunately merely added to excess capacity in the economy. Purchases of such equipment provided jobs for foreign workers, but the equipment itself ended up in the Philippines as industrial monuments.

AN EVALUATION OF PHILIPPINE DEVELOPMENT POLICIES

In judging a country's development performance, four economic criteria are relevant. How well did the country succeed in raising its growth rate? To what extent was the country successful in solving the problems of unemployment and underemployment? Did the development effort help to distribute income more equitably? Were resources allocated more efficiently because of the development programs? When these criteria are applied to the Philippines, it would appear that the country does not receive very high marks.

The main objective of trade, fiscal, and monetary policies in the 1950s was to accelerate the rate of industrial growth. As already mentioned, while it is not easy to separate the type of "catch-up" growth that would be expected after World War II from development that occurred in response to deliberate policies, a reasonable conclusion is that industrial growth was significantly accelerated during this decade by the import-substitution policies of the government. However, once the relatively easy type of import substitution was completed, by the latter part of the 1950s, the development rate in the manufacturing sector as well as in the economy as a whole declined quite sharply. During the decontrol period from 1960 to 1965 that followed this slowdown, the growth rates for manufactures and real gross national product fell even lower. Not until the 1966–69 period did these development rates return to the level of the late 1950s. But even the growth rates in this period could not be maintained for long. Thus the question arises as to whether different sorts of development policies would have brought about higher rates of growth.

One study throwing some light on this subject is the investigation by Gonzalo Jurado into the production cost of exchange controls in 1961.[39] Using linear programming techniques and comparing actual production levels with those that would exist under free trade, Jurado estimated the production cost of exchange controls in 1961 to be between 0.18 per cent and 1.65 per cent of gross national product. Presumably one would wish to balance the dynamic benefits from import substitution, especially in the early 1950s, against this static allocation loss, which became relatively more important after the reduction in growth rates in the latter part of the 1950s. While any assessment of the net balance of these factors can be no more than an educated guess, my view is that it is not obvious that the government's development policies, as compared with free trade, increased the growth rate over the entire 1949–71 period.

A more relevant assessment, however, would involve a comparison of the government's import-substitution policies with a set of policies designed to stimulate more export growth, particularly in the manufacturing area. In other words, the government might have tried to adopt at least some of the export-oriented policies of Korea and Taiwan. This does not mean that no import substitution should have occurred. Undoubtedly, the government's action of protecting and subsidizing some industries did help to overcome various market imperfections and correct for various technological externalities in ways that improved the dynamic allocation of resources. Yet these policies were pushed too far, and it is now difficult politically and economically to dismantle the inefficient parts of the industrial system. These parts of the industrial system also retard potential export growth in manufacturing by being able to bid away scarce resources from this sector. A more selective use of import-substituting and export-promoting policies might have resulted in faster growth in the past and almost certainly would have set the basis for a higher development rate in the future than the inward-looking policy of import substitution. Fortunately, within recent years more emphasis has been placed on stimulating exports, though probably not yet enough to establish a firm foundation for future growth.

While one's judgment of the Philippine economy between 1949 and 1971 on the basis of the growth criterion is likely to be uncertain, an assessment of the country's performance according to the other three criteria seems quite straightforward. The economy has not done well on the basis of any of these criteria. The distortions in resource allocation were examined in detail in

Chapter 5 and in the first section of this chapter. The bias produced by the trading regimes toward capital-intensive production and thus the low rate of employment creation associated with the country's growth have also been discussed in the first section of this chapter. Finally, the failure of the real wages of labor to be any higher currently than at the beginning of the development efforts and the high profits fostered by import controls have been analyzed in the preceding section and in the last chapter. Consequently, considering all the criteria and viewing the 1949–71 period as a whole, it seems necessary to conclude that the economic policies pursued by the government did not make the needed contribution to the solution of the country's problems.

THE POLITICAL CLIMATE
OF DEVELOPMENT

Perhaps the most serious threat to the use of the economic surplus available in the Philippines for steady development is its dissipation for short-run political purposes. As has been mentioned several times in Chapters 2, 3, and 4, monetary and fiscal policies have been closely related to the two-year election cycle. A study of the 1957–68 period by Averich, Denton, and Koehler showed, for example, that in the five election years in this period, the change in government net receipts from the previous year was negative, whereas in six of the nonelection years the change was positive in five years and negative in one.[40] If 1969 is added, another negative change is given for net receipts of the government in an election year. The authors also show that expansionary and contractionary monetary policies are closely related to the election cycle. They further point out that these monetary and fiscal policies produce alternating increases and decreases in the real growth rate of GNP as well as periodic exchange crises. On the last point they conclude that periodic exchange crises "at any level of foreign exchange availability are inevitable with the electioneering practices." [41]

Although it seems to me that Averich, Denton, and Koehler do not give sufficient emphasis to the growth goals of the government in accounting for fiscal, monetary, and foreign-exchange developments, there is no doubt that the practice of increasing government expenditures and easing monetary control in an election year has greatly contributed to the nation's economic problems. The 1969 foreign-exchange crisis is a case in point. Only some fortunate development such as a sharp rise in export prices could have prevented an eventual exchange crisis, but large increases in government spending and the money supply brought about the crisis much sooner than it would otherwise have occurred and made it more severe. Now that the country's economy is so dependent on foreign trade for essential imports, a severe exchange crisis imposes significant hardships on the urban sector. The strikes and riots of 1970–71 attest to the penalties imposed on labor.

The Philippine economy possesses favorable basic conditions for growth. Traditional exports coupled with the growing importance of new mineral and agricultural exports should provide adequate foreign-exchange resources for sustaining a satisfactory rate of growth. The demonstrated savings and entrepreneurial ability of the population also should prevent a lack of capital or business talent from becoming serious obstacles to satisfactory growth. However, the main driving forces for sustaining development will have to come from the internal economic interactions among the various sectors. The foreign sector can play an important role in facilitating this growth, but the easy days of import substitution are over. Moreover, trying to force the domestic production of manufactured intermediates and capital goods in the manner used to achieve local production of simply processed consumer goods is likely to prove self-defeating because of the greater import requirements for the former and the adverse effects on exports. What is needed is a more realistic policy of development that does not aim at the establishment of a completely integrated industrial structure in the not-too-distant future, but instead gives greater emphasis to export production and high employment in light manufactures and services in the industrial sector. Yet, no change in development policies will prevent periodic economic crises unless the government exercises a much greater degree of fiscal and monetary discipline.

NOTES

1. The detailed 1960 breakdown of the manufacturing sector is not presented here because of the length of the table.

2. See the section on Growth Effects, in this chapter, for a further analysis of the behavior of the output-capital (or capital-output) ratio.

3. However, if it were not for the very high wage rate in the beverages industry, these ratios would also show a rise between 1948 and 1956. Specifically, if this industry is excluded, average earnings are P1,950 in 1938, P1,869 in 1948, P2,026 in 1956, and P2,019 in 1960. Jeffrey G. Williamson, "Economic Growth in the Philippines, 1947–1965: The Role of Traditional Inputs, Education and Technical Change" (Institute of Economic Development and Research, School of Economics, University of the Philippines, Discussion Paper 67–8, 1970), found that about one-tenth of the aggregate growth rate can be explained by investment in education.

4. The figures for the decline between 1960 and 1964—from 0.25 to 0.15—are, however, suspect. In Table 6-8, for example, it is indicated that the capital-goods share of imports declined only from 19.7 per cent in the 1959–61 period to 17.4 per cent in the 1963–65 period.

5. Mahar Mangahas, "A Broad View of the Philippine Employment Problem" [Paper presented at a seminar on Employment Creation Strategies for Southeast Asian

Economies, sponsored by the Southeast Asian Development Advisory Group (SEADAG) of the Asia Society, Atlanta, December 7–10, 1972]. The data in the rest of the paragraph are from this paper.

6. Ibid., p. 7.

7. From Mahar Mangahas, William H. Meyer, and R. Barker, *Labor Absorption in Philippine Agriculture* (Paris: Organization for Economic Cooperation and Development, 1972); and Harry T. Oshima, "Labor Absorption in East and Southeast Asia," *Malayan Economic Review*, October 1972, as reported in ibid., p. 9.

8. George L. Hicks and Geoffrey McNicoll, *Trade and Growth in the Philippines* (Ithaca: Cornell University Press, 1971), p. 68.

9. *Philippine Sugar Handbook* (Manila: Sugar News Press, 1970), pp. 13–14. The following data on the quota system are also from this source.

10. Hicks and McNicoll, *Trade and Growth*, pp. 194–195.

11. Lee Douglas Badgett, "The Response of Processing Activity to Preferential Tariff Reductions: The Philippines Case, 1900 to 1940" (Ph.D. diss., Yale University, 1971), p. 182.

12. National Economic Council, *Four-Year Development Plan*, Fiscal-Years 1971–74 (Manila: Office of the President, 1970), p. 58.

13. Ibid., pp. 58–59; also based on conversations with officials of the Development Bank of the Philippines.

14. The following equations are from Romeo M. Bautista and Jose Encarnación, Jr., "A Foreign Trade Submodel of the Philippine Economy, 1950–1969" (University of the Philippines, School of Economics, Institute of Economic Development and Research, Discussion Paper 71–28, December 1971). The domestic output of coconuts is considered a predetermined variable in their model. Numbers in parentheses below the regression coefficients are the corresponding t values. Annual data were used for the years covered.

15. Jose Encarnación and others, *Econometric Models of the Philippines* (Manila: National Economic Council, 1970), Chap. 6.

16. Loc. cit.

17. See Hicks and McNicoll, *Trade and Growth*, pp. 211–215, for a more extensive discussion of this problem.

18. Cited in ibid., p. 215.

19. Philippine Association for Permanent Forests, Inc., *Philippine Forestry and Wood Industry* (Diliman, Quezon City: PERMAFOR, 1972), p. 34.

20. The logic of using the sum of export prices is that output is a function of the capital stock which in turn is a function of investment in previous years. Investment in any previous year depends on the price of copper in that year.

21. Encarnación and others, *Econometric Models*, p. 18.

22. The proportionate increase in the quantity of exports of any commodity is given by multiplying the relevant supply elasticity by the proportionate increase in the peso price of the commodity. Since the dollar price of the commodity is assumed to remain constant, multiplying this proportionate increase by the average annual dollar export value of the commodity during the period gives the hypothetical dollar increase in exports.

23. Gerardo P. Sicat, *Economic Policy and Philippine Development* (Quezon City: University of Philippines Press, 1972), Chap. 9.

24. Richard W. Hooley and Gerardo P. Sicat, "Investment Demand in Philippine Manufacturing" (University of the Philippines, School of Economics, Institute of Economic Development and Research, Discussion Paper 67-2, 1967).

25. Ibid., pp. 47–49.

26. The yearly figures are obtained by dividing the difference in GDP between two successive years into the volume of gross domestic capital formation in the later year. The ratios for 1948–49, 1951–52, and 1966–67 are combined with those for one year later because these ratios were abnormally high. The source of the data, which are in real terms, is the national accounts of the Philippines as given by the Office of Statistical Coordination and Standards of the National Economic Council and reported in various issues of the *Statistical Reporter.*

27. The ratios refer to changes in the real value of fixed assets and real value added between the given date and two years prior to the given date. The years 1966 and 1968 are combined because of unusually high and low ratios, i.e., 3.27 and 0.50, respectively. The source of the data is Philippine Bureau of Census and Statistics, *Preliminary Report on the BCS Annual Survey of Manufactures, 1968* (Manila, 1970). The earliest survey of manufacturing is for 1956.

28. See John J. Carrol, *The Filipino Manufacturing Entrepreneur* (Ithaca: Cornell University Press, 1965); and F. H. Golay, *The Philippines: Public Policy and National Economic Development* (Ithaca: Cornell University Press, 1961), pp. 408–409.

29. Williamson, "Economic Growth in the Philippines."

30. These figures and the following figures are from ibid., p. 25. Williamson's assumption B data are reported here.

31. Loc. cit., p. 21.

32. As reported in A. V. H. Hartendorp, *History of Industry and Trade in the Philippines; the Magsaysay Administration* (Manila: Philippine Education Press, 1961), pp. 444–445.

33. Ibid., pp. 445–448.

34. For an application of this framework to the Philippines, see Hicks and McNicoll, *Trade and Growth.*

35. Marvin C. Goodstein, "The Pace and Pattern of Philippine Economic Growth" (Cornell University, Department of Asian Studies, Data Paper 48, July 1962; mimeo.).

36. See Hicks and McNicoll, *Trade and Growth,* pp. 76–87.

37. Hicks and McNicoll, *Trade and Growth,* p. 91.

38. Vicente B. Valdepeñas, Jr., *The Protection and Development of Philippine Manufacturing* (Manila: Ateneo University Press, 1970), p. 14.

39. Gonzalo M. Jurado, "The Production Cost of Exchange Control in the Philippines, 1961" (University of the Philippines, School of Economics, Institute of Economic Development and Research, Discussion Paper 71-16, 1971). Also Jurado, "A Linear Programming Analysis of the Economic Cost of Exchange Control: The Philippine Case" (Ph.D. diss., University of Wisconsin, 1970).

40. H. S. Averich, F. H. Denton, and J. E. Koehler, *A Crisis of Ambiguity: Political and Economic Development in the Philippines,* A Report Prepared for the Agency for International Development (Santa Monica, Calif.: RAND Corp., 1970), p. 162.

41. Ibid., p. 170.

Appendixes

Appendix A

Definition of Concepts and Delineation of Phases

DEFINITION OF CONCEPTS USED IN THE PROJECT

Exchange Rates.

1. *Nominal exchange rate:* The official parity for a transaction. For countries maintaining a single exchange rate registered with the International Monetary Fund, the nominal exchange rate is the registered rate.

2. *Effective exchange rate (EER):* The number of units of local currency actually paid or received for a one-dollar international transaction. Surcharges, tariffs, the implicit interest foregone on guarantee deposits, and any other charges against purchases of goods and services abroad are included, as are rebates, the value of import replenishment rights, and other incentives to earn foreign exchange for sales of goods and services abroad.

3. *Price-level-deflated (PLD) nominal exchange rates:* The nominal exchange rate deflated in relation to some base period by the price level index of the country.

4. *Price-level-deflated EER (PLD-EER):* The EER deflated by the price level index of the country.

5. *Purchasing-power-parity adjusted exchange rates:* The relevant (nominal or effective) exchange rate multiplied by the ratio of the foreign price level to the domestic price level.

157

Devaluation.

1. *Gross devaluation:* The change in the parity registered with the IMF (or, synonymously in most cases, de jure devaluation).

2. *Net devaluation:* The weighted average of changes in EERs by classes of transactions (or, synonymously in most cases, de facto devaluation).

3. *Real gross devaluation:* The gross devaluation adjusted for the increase in the domestic price level over the relevant period.

4. *Real net devaluation:* The net devaluation similarly adjusted.

Protection Concepts.

1. *Explicit tariff:* The amount of tariff charged against the import of a good as a percentage of the import price (in local currency at the nominal exchange rate) of the good.

2. *Implicit tariff* (or, synonymously, tariff equivalent): The ratio of the domestic price (net of normal distribution costs) minus the c.i.f. import price to the c.i.f. import price in local currency.

3. *Premium:* The windfall profit accruing to the recipient of an import license per dollar of imports. It is the difference between the domestic selling price (net of normal distribution costs) and the landed cost of the item (including tariffs and other charges). The premium is thus the difference between the implicit and the explicit tariff (including other charges) multiplied by the nominal exchange rate.

4. *Nominal tariff:* The tariff—either explicit or implicit as specified—on a commodity.

5. *Effective tariff:* The explicit or implicit tariff on value added as distinct from the nominal tariff on a commodity. This concept is also expressed as the effective rate of protection (ERP) or as the effective protective rate (EPR).

6. *Domestic resources costs (DRC):* The value of domestic resources (evaluated at "shadow" or opportunity cost prices) employed in earning or saving a dollar of foreign exchange (in the value-added sense) when producing domestic goods.

DELINEATION OF PHASES USED IN TRACING THE EVOLUTION OF EXCHANGE CONTROL REGIMES

To achieve comparability of analysis among different countries, each author of a country study was asked to identify the chronological development of his country's payments regime through the following phases. There was no presumption that a country would necessarily pass through all the phases in chronological sequence.

Phase I: During this period, quantitative restrictions on international transactions are imposed and then intensified. They generally are initiated in response to an unsustainable payments deficit and then, for a period, are intensified. During the period when reliance upon quantitative restrictions as a means of controlling the balance of payments is increasing, the country is said to be in Phase I.

Phase II: During this phase, quantitative restrictions are still intense, but various price measures are taken to offset some of the undesired results of the system. Heightened tariffs, surcharges on imports, rebates for exports, special tourist exchange rates, and other price interventions are used in this phase. However, primary reliance continues to be placed on quantitative restrictions.

Phase III: This phase is characterized by an attempt to systematize the changes which take place during Phase II. It generally starts with a formal exchange-rate change and may be accompanied by removal of some of the surcharges, etc., imposed during Phase II and by reduced reliance upon quantitative restrictions. Phase III may be little more than a tidying-up operation (in which case the likelihood is that the country will re-enter Phase II), or it may signal the beginning of withdrawal from reliance upon quantitative restrictions.

Phase IV: If the changes in Phase III result in adjustments within the country, so that liberalization can continue, the country is said to enter Phase IV. The necessary adjustments generally include increased foreign-exchange earnings and gradual relaxation of quantitative restrictions. The latter relaxation may take the form of changes in the nature of quantitative restrictions or of increased foreign-exchange allocations, and thus reduced premiums, under the same administrative system.

Phase V: This is a period during which an exchange regime is fully liberalized. There is full convertibility on current account, and quantitative restrictions are not employed as a means of regulating the ex ante balance of payments.

Appendix B

Important Philippine Names and Abbreviations

BOI: Board of Investment

DBP: Development Bank of the Philippines, successor to the Rehabilitation Finance Corporation; makes loans to industry, agriculture, and the government at levels below the free-market rate

Import Control Board: established to regulate imports under the Import Control Act of 1948

NEC: National Economic Council

RFC: Rehabilitation Finance Corporation

Presidents of the Philippines: Elpidio Quirino: April 15, 1948, to December 31, 1953; Ramon Magsaysay: January 1, 1954, to March 17, 1957; Carlos Garcia: March 17, 1957, to December 31, 1961; Diosdado Macapagal: January 1, 1962, to December 31, 1965; Ferdinand Marcos: since January 1, 1966

Bell Trade Act (1946): stipulates schedule for the elimination of preferential treatment between the United States and the Philippines

Laurel-Langley Agreement (1955): revises scheduled rate of preferential treatment between the United States and the Philippines

Index

161